As Sue talks you through each cha[ ] enough to do—she opens the windows of her sou[ ] poems, she points the way to deeper intimacy with Jesus. Drink deeply here according to the thirst of your soul. Allow the paths of this book to guide you into deeper relationship with our Lord Jesus.

Bob Sorge, author, *Secrets of the Secret Place*

With sensitivity and depth of insight that can only come from someone who has walked a difficult, lonely road, Sue Popa pulls the curtain back on her personal journey from self-loathing and despair to hope and healing through her relationship with Jesus. I had the honor of walking that road with Sue for several years, so reading her intimate poems and piercing observations was both emotional and exhilarating. For all who wonder, "Does my life really matter?" this book is for you.

Dr. Nick Twomey, Traverse City, MI

Whispers through the Lattice: Discovering the Romance of the Gospel is a truly unique, poetic, inspirational picture of God's tender love and great affection for His creation. Susan uses the good news of the gospel along with her openness, vulnerability and personal experiences to draw one into Jesus' amazing love and healing. She brings insight into your paradigm of the Divine Romancer that will melt your heart to bring heart liberation, healing, revival, renewal and restoration from fear, shame, pain, sin, loneliness and brokenness. An essential read for you and your group to be impacted by the gospel as you are challenged in each chapter with heart-provoking questions to go a step deeper. Holy Spirit will reveal your original design and the love of Jesus, stirring a heart hunger and drawing you into an intimate healing relationship with the Divine Lover.

Rebecca Stontz, Co-Director, *Youth With A Mission*, Traverse City Missionary to Iraq, Romania, Turkey

Susan Popa has crafted a narrative of poetry and testimony showing God's grace and love available to all of us traveling life's highway. Readers will find each chapter addresses another aspect of our lives and allows the Spirit to speak to us in various ways enhancing our own growth and development. Reading her story shows there are messages specifically designed for each of us. Thank you, Susan, for allowing us another opportunity to grow in Him.

Charlene A. Lutes, Ph.D., Author

Being familiar with Susan's touched-by-God writings, I have been anxiously waiting for her manuscript to become a book-in-my-hand devotional. Actually, I did not wait patiently; I used an unpublished portion of her work for a Christian women's retreat. There our hearts were awakened by the images her words inspired. Her poetic renderings brought us into a greater understanding of God's love, forgiveness, and provision. I have a special place for *Whispers through the Lattice*; it stands with my collection of spiritually gifted authors.

Susanne Box Elenbaas, Spiritual Encouragement Essayist: www. hopelessly-hopeful.com

I had the pleasure of working with Sue Popa on this beautiful devotional book. It is a lovely and courageous book written to expose the lies of life's struggles and the truth of God's everlasting love. We can all resonate with Sue's honesty, and know we are valued and desired by our Lover and Bridegroom who knows us intimately.

Rev. Peggy Byland, newspaper columnist and contributor to *Words of Hope: International Media Ministry*

Whispers through the Lattice: Discovering the Romance of the Gospel intertwines poetry with the personal stories that prompted each poem...a lyrical expression of Sue's heart. There is a refreshing transparency wrapped around her life experiences which permeates each story and poem. All are accompanied with correlating scripture verses. *Whispers through the Lattice* is a unique book which invites readers to seek further intimacy with God and along the way, receive healing to spirit and soul.

Marjorie Long, Executive Director and Founder of the non-profit ministry *Gloria in Excelsis Deo*

Relatable life stories clearly pointing to an applied Biblical truth are blended together with a powerful poetic gift making this book not only a delight to read but also a case for pause... to stop and consider... to reflect, to draw near and listen to the Voice that speaks of eternal affection for us. I especially appreciate the lesson from the snake and the rock in chapter 12; so practical and instructional. Thank you for sharing your gift with us Susan.

I highly recommend this book for men and women alike who desire a moment of pause to listen to the Beloved.

Pastor Jim Roe (retired), Traverse City, Michigan

Of the many things I admire about my beautiful friend Sue, two of the most striking are her deep love of God's Word and her passion for worship and His intimate presence. I told her once: "God will make you fearless in worship." Raising a large family and experiencing years of gut-wrenching family trauma, at times it seemed life fought viciously against her intense desire to worship God. Sue's gentle nature belies a fierce determination to persevere through incredible trials which would have felled a lesser person, yet have sweetened her nature and built layers of wisdom only endurance through such trials can produce. God has taught her many rich lessons as she clung to Him in desperate situations and found Him full of love and acceptance and utterly faithful. If knowing you are deeply loved makes you brave, Sue has indeed become that fearless worshiper!

Julie Elliott-Eickenroth, Founder of *HeartSkills Coaching,* Founder/ Executive Director of *Freedom Farm Ministries Grand Traverse, Inc.*

Whispers through the Lattice:

Discovering the Romance

of the Gospel

by

Susan Popa

Published by Mission Point Press
2554 Chandler Rd.
Traverse City, MI 49686
231) 421-9513
www.MissionPointPress.com

ISBN: 978-1-943995-80-6
Library of Congress Control Number: 2018951516

Printed in the United States of America.

Cover art by Jan Bower. Cover design by Gary Bower.
Interior illustration by Louise Bass. Author photo by Rebekah Popa.

For my children —

Isaac, Hannah, Rebekah, Joshua, and Simeon...

May you hear the whispers of the true Lover of your souls,

and may you fall ever more deeply in love with Him.

And...

for all those who long to see beyond the lattice.

Table of Contents

By God's grace we are....

ACKNOWLEDGMENTS

I would like to express my utmost thanks to...

- *Jesus — for setting Your affection on me, washing me clean and drawing me to Your heart.*
- *Holy Spirit — for breathing upon my heart as we created together. You make writing my delight!*
- *Mom and Dad (John and Jan Dyksterhouse) — for first introducing me to Jesus, for instilling in me a love for poetry and books, and for embodying for me an amazing picture of the father-heart of God.*
- *Brian, my dear husband — for tenderly loving me. Thank-you for encouraging me to pursue writing and for patiently and sacrificially providing me the time to complete this work.*
- *Rev. Peggy Byland, my editor — for believing in me and in this book. I may never have finished this race without you giving me a second wind. Your expert editing skills have been invaluable.*
- *Dr. Charlene Lutes — for your early editing suggestions which helped me learn to more effectively tell my story.*
- *Julie Elliott-Eickenroth — for valuing my poetry and giving me courage to step into the light.*
- *Louise Bass, Starr Barker, Myra Boone, Susanne Elenbaas, Linda Cichocky, Tina Neihardt and Nedra Shoobridge — for reading my early manuscripts and giving feedback and encouragement.*
- *Heather Shaw and Aimé Merizon of Mission Point Press — for patiently polishing all the rough edges and pulling these words together in a beautiful format.*

Special thanks to the many treasured friends who have prayed this book into being.

~ Sue Popa

"However, I consider my life worth nothing to me; my only aim is to finish the race and complete the task the Lord Jesus has given me—the task of testifying to the good news of God's grace."

Acts 20:24

INTRODUCTION

WHEN I FIRST MET Jesus Christ as a young child, it was like stepping into an ocean. I grew up in Michigan, but I remember dreaming about the ocean and then eventually traveling there with my parents. When I took those first delightful steps in, the wetness lapped across my bare toes, the salt spray seeped into my mouth and saturated my taste buds. I was surrounded by the roaring waves and the sense of wonder and freedom and power.

But I had not yet even begun to know that ocean, to explore the deep and find the treasure chests hidden in secret caverns. I could recall accounts I'd read in science books, or photos I'd seen in *National Geographic* that gave a one-dimensional testimony to the existence of an immense underwater wilderness, but I had no true concept of the thousands of multicolored creatures teeming with life beneath the waves. One can learn only so much from a book. Beyond the shore, thousands of feet down, hidden in the cold, vast darkness lay underwater corals, sea creatures and forests. Each new depth could reveal new beauties, new life forms previously untouched, unseen.

How could I even begin to know the ocean? And yet Jesus beckons me in to know Him. With the pull of each receding wave as I stand in the shallow water, I can hear Him saying, "Deeper! Come in and know me!" The Ocean is amazing even on the shore, but oh...there's more. Eventually, if I am going to explore this Ocean, I will have to get out where my feet can't touch at all.

"You will seek me and find me when you seek me with all your heart." (Jeremiah 29:13) As we seek to know God, He *will* reveal Himself to us, incrementally, like the steps of a journey into the ocean. And His desire for us is that at some point along the journey we will

actually fall in love with that Ocean. As John and Stasi Eldredge say in their book *Captivating,* "Christianity changes dramatically when we discover that it, too, is a great romance." (Thomas Nelson, Inc., 04/07/2005, p. 29)

Discovering that great romance has been the most life changing discovery of my life, leading me out of self-hatred, shame, emotionally dependent relationships, and the bondage of an eating disorder. It has been my lifeline through depression, helping me forgive and feel loved. It has been my comfort in the grief of watching my sons struggle through alcoholism and drug addiction, and it has released my heart from the guilt of parenting failures. This great romance has given me times of joy that go way deeper than any other joy I've experienced. This book is my story, but it is really all about Jesus.

Whispers through the Lattice is an unfolding of 32 scripture-based poems, woven together with prose, into 28 chapters, each proclaiming some aspect of the gospel (good news) of God's grace given to us in the person of Jesus Christ. The introductions to each poem provide background information that make the poems more meaningful. The scriptures that inspired the poems are noted beneath their titles and frequent action steps, with open spaces for journaling, suggest ways one may pursue a greater depth of relationship with God. Included in an appendix at the back of the book are chapter-by-chapter questions that could be used for small group discussion.

I am striving to be honest about my experience of the Christian life. As I have prepared these pages I have at times felt overwhelmed with the reality of not being able to live up to unwavering faith in the truth of what I have written. I am like a rough clay vase filled with the living water that Jesus spoke of in John 7:38, and my desire is to tip over and spill out, even in my awkwardness, some of the glorious truths God has given us.

The good news of the gospel is that all these chapters, these aspects of God's grace, are constantly true whether I feel like they are or not. I am weak and still broken in many ways and yet the truth of the gospel does not depend on my ability to hold onto it. I have a Savior, Jesus Christ, who holds onto me.

I also have an enemy. *"Your enemy the devil prowls around like a roaring lion looking for someone to devour." (1Peter 5:8b)* I think this enemy of my soul would want me to think I need to have my act together before I can boldly proclaim the truth of the Gospel of Jesus Christ...because he knows I'll never get there until I see Jesus face-to-face, and then it will be too late. I refuse to give him that pleasure.

The good news of the gospel is that I am set free to be bold. As a believer in Jesus Christ, a beloved child of the Living God, I have the Holy Spirit alive in me, roaring like a lion. Despite my weakness, this uncontainable fountain of glorious living water is mine to spill out with the reckless joy of a child unleashing a puppy as I race down the seashore and splash into the waves. God has given me something way too wonderful to pour out politely from a china teapot.

Revelation

"The unfolding of your words gives light..."
Psalm 119:130

Within the pages of His Book wait rows of folded words.
Like white shirts carefully prepared
They wait there to be heard.
Hidden deep within each word, each one bears my name.
He embroidered them in red when for my soul He came.
At first glance I see only words,
But if I take the time
Unfolding brings the light to see my name—
These words are mine!

* Note: Each of the chapters that follow hold out to you a stack of folded words. May you delight in unfolding them and find your name within each one. Scattered throughout the chapters wait extra spaces for you to journal a record of the light God gives you. I pray that God *"...may give you the Spirit of wisdom and revelation so that you may know him better." Ephesians 1:17*

Chapter 1

FEARLESS

IF YOU KNEW ME in my younger years you would probably have considered me highly unlikely to live fearlessly. I was the child in the Sunday school program who asked her teacher if she could say her dreaded lines with a bag over her head. To say I have been paralyzed by fear is an understatement. My natural tendency is to hide, to be silent, to stay in the background where I feel safe.

And so, as I found myself preparing to share my life story with a group of troubled teens and the staff at House of Hope in Traverse City, Michigan, I felt miles away from my comfort zone. I was invited to come as a guest speaker to share how God had led me out of years of depression and bulimia.

Riding in the car one night, as this speaking engagement drew near, I was captured by the sight of a bonfire in the distance. Something about it drew me in and I sensed God speaking to me through it, calling me to be a bonfire in the night for these teens I would address. The broken pieces of my life would be like the broken pieces of wood that fueled that fire. I didn't have to be the fire; I didn't have to make the light. I just had to offer up my story and allow the Holy Spirit to ignite the fire that would bring light to these teens who needed light in their darkness.

It was out of this revelation that the poem "No Longer Tame" was born. "No Longer Tame" speaks of the gift of fearlessness that God held out to me, a fearlessness that was growing out of ever-deepening trust in Jesus. The scripture on which this poem is based gives us a window into Jesus' anger when people who wanted to draw near to Him were prevented from doing so.

"When it was almost time for the Jewish Passover, Jesus went up to Jerusalem. In the temple courts he found people selling cattle, sheep and doves, and others sitting at tables exchanging money. So, he made a whip out of cords, and drove all from the temple courts, both sheep and cattle; he scattered the coins of the money changers and overturned their tables. To those who sold doves he said, "Get these out of here! Stop turning my Father's house into a market!" His disciples remembered that it is written: "Zeal for your house will consume me." John 2:13-17

What angers us most, reveals what we care about most. Jesus cares most about being with His children. His love is not a weak thing. It is not passive and sweet. It flows out of a raging fire of powerful, passionate jealousy. Jesus wants us. His desire is intense. This is where our security is rooted.

A turning point in my life occurred years ago when my children were 1, 3, 5 and 7 years old (a fifth child came four years later). Though my children were the joy of my life, the stress of home-schooling and raising four active children so close in age was immense. One exhausting day after securing a babysitter, I drove to the grocery store, and as was my pattern, bought a package of cookies. Sitting in the parking lot I de-stressed by methodically consuming one chewier-than-I-thought cookie after another. The fleeting comfort of sugar eased my anxiety for a moment but was soon overcome by the guilt of turning once again to food to fill the void that I innately knew should be filled by God.

At this point I already suffered from TMJ, the stress-related inflammation of my jaw joints, and the strain placed upon these joints by that day's hard chewing injured them further. In the following weeks and months, I would be reduced to a near-liquid diet and hours of physical therapy as I attempted to regain strength in my jaw. With my coping mechanism now limited, the reality that I did not know how to find peace in God rose to the surface.

Lying on the living room floor in the dark one night, with my family asleep and the quietness allowing the void in my heart to engulf me, I cried out to God. "There must be more to knowing You than I am experiencing. I believe in You. I've been a Christian for many years now, but I feel like I barely know You." This marked the beginning of a voracious, all-consuming hunger to know God that would lead me to seek Him with all my heart.

A few months later my husband and I felt the LORD leading us to a different church. We left the church I loved, in which I had grown up, where I had received years of sound Biblical teaching and solid relationships, a church that gave me deep roots in the faith, and we entered a church where one thing drew me - the worship.

These people were singing directly *to* God, more than singing *about* Him. Entering the sanctuary, I felt unnoticed. Surrounding me were people with eyes closed, hands raised, some kneeling, some dancing, engaged in an intimacy of worship that awakened in me an intense longing for more of God. It was here, as I closed my eyes and began to open my heart in worship to God, that the shame I carried in my heart was exposed. I knew God loved me as part of the lost world He died for, but there were still mountains of fear standing between Him and me, fear that He didn't really *like* me, that He didn't really *want* me to come to Him.

I remember many Sundays hurrying out of the sanctuary, mid-service, to escape into a bathroom stall in tears, unable to see beyond those mountains of fear and the volcanic shame welling up within them. During this time a friend told me, "God is going to make you fearless in worship." Years later now I would say yes, He has done this for me. Not to the full extent that I will experience in heaven, but I now know the joy of approaching God in freedom and confidence, trusting that He delights to see me coming. This is the gospel!

I hope that as I share some of the steps of my journey deeper into the knowledge of God, that the broken pieces of my life will be the fuel that brings you light.

No Longer Tame

John 2:13-17, 1 John 4:4, Romans 15:13

Here I stand before you now
A bonfire in the night
The broken pieces of my life
The fuel that brings you light.
Hope-tongues dance up through the dark
Spirit burn a contrast stark
Dispel the lies that God is dead
Shout the truth of hope instead.
Though fear may try to silence me
It can't smother the flame.
The Fire in me is greater
Crackling sparks no longer tame
Shoot out in each direction
Raging Fire of Salvation.
A whip scatters the blackness
The God of Hope is zealous.

A Step Deeper In...

"My shield is God Most High, who saves the upright in heart. God is a righteous judge who displays His wrath every day." Psalm 7:10, 11

As I recently read this, I realized these are verses I've just brushed over all my life, not letting the weight of them sink in. *Every day* God displays His wrath. This is not a pansy God we are running to. Every day God throws Himself between me and the enemy of my soul, as my shield. It's like He roars and shouts, "She's Mine! You can never have her!"

David is one of the authors of the book of Psalms. His fearless confidence in the LORD came from knowing the depth of security he possessed because of God's actively fighting on his behalf every day.

This is where the gospel of God's grace begins. Jesus is zealous for me. It's not just that He had mercy on me to forgive my sins, like a judge in a courtroom. That itself is wonderful, but it's much more exciting than that. Jesus actually *desires* me, enough to get angry when something or someone is blocking me from being with Him.

What is it in your life that blocks you from experiencing intimacy with Jesus? If Jesus were writing this, He would invite you to ask Him what it is. The main way God "scatters the blackness" in my life is through His Word.

Take time to meditate on the verses beneath the title of this poem. Pray for Jesus to reveal Himself to you as the God who is zealous for you personally. Ask Him to show you anything that holds you back from true intimacy with Him, and then ask Him to remove whatever barriers He shows you.

Chapter 2

BEAUTIFUL

ONCE I GET A GLIMPSE of the beautiful God who is jealous for me and zealous for winning my heart and drawing me close to Him, a question bursts out of my soul... WHY? Why would God want me?

Why does a man pursue a woman? She is beautiful to Him. That is the bottom line. He is attracted to her beauty. And this union of one man and one woman in marriage is the picture God has given us to portray symbolically this type of total intimacy He wants with us. This romance is in our DNA.

Good fairy tales revolve around romance. Little girls dream of being princesses and little boys dream of being strong heroes. There is a real-life fairy tale that is too good to be true — but it *is* true. We *are* the beautiful princesses loved by the Prince!

Oh, how I have struggled to take this in, to hold it firmly in my hand before it slips away again like a slippery bar of soap. Sometimes I've held it quite a while, forgetting even that it was there, only to wake up one morning realizing it had slipped away, my hand left holding mere soap suds, a remnant of faith in a Lover who is ravished by my beauty.

And then my search begins again. "Jesus, I want to know You. I want to taste again the sweetness of how you feel about me." And He promises that when I ask, He will answer, and when I seek Him I will find Him. He seems to love this game of hide and seek, this process of watching me discover Him.

I struggled with an eating disorder for many years and so my sense of ugliness was deeply ingrained. The desire to be beautiful controlled my life. But beyond physical beauty, I longed for true inner beauty.

One Sunday, my husband Brian and I had a fight on the way to church, and I entered the sanctuary feeling totally unworthy to worship God. I was overwhelmed with my inability to love my husband. My selfishness and pride were insurmountable.

I sat in the back alone, covered in shame, praying God would come to me. At that moment, a dear friend felt she needed to move to the other side of the room and she now stood right behind me. Without even knowing of my struggle she had felt moved to come and sit with me. She put her arm around me and said, "I think that if God would want to speak to you He'd send a part of His Body to just sit by you and hold your hand and enjoy you like this."

I knew God had answered my heart's cry and sent her to pour out His mercy on me. I shared my struggle and she prayed with me. During prayer, she had a vision of me as a beautiful swan.

That evening or the next, in an effort to find connection with Brian again, I sat down next to him as he was flipping through the TV channels. I almost never watch TV. But I soon knew this was where God wanted me because the show Brian settled on was called "The Swan." I had been pondering that vision and here God was giving me revelation about it through the TV of all things!

The show was about women who were chosen to be in an extreme makeover program for the summer. They were provided with plastic surgery, exercise programs, beauty treatments and counseling, all designed to transform them into strikingly beautiful women. The women could not see themselves all summer until the end when they would stand before a huge curtained mirror, and when they were ready, the curtain would be drawn open and they would finally see themselves in this mirror, as the beautiful women they had become.

The episode that was airing that night featured one woman's story and I knew God was showing me myself and what He is doing in my life and what He sees in me. The featured woman's life symbolized my own. She was burned in a house fire as a young child. Covered in scars, especially on her cheeks, she spent her lifetime hiding her face. She was quiet and had a sweet humble spirit about her, but a deep sadness and shame dominated her life.

One scene from the program stood out to me. The woman was lying on the operating table awaiting plastic surgery to fix her scars. The surgeon so tenderly touched her cheeks and said, "Oh, I see beauty here!"

I have heard it taught that in scripture the cheeks are symbolic of our emotions. The woman's scars were on her cheeks. They were her source of shame. This too has been my source of shame— not my face, but my emotions.

Since childhood I have struggled with depression and have felt much shame over not having emotional stability. God has been working deep healing in my emotions, and I know that He is transforming me into a beautiful swan, His bride.

But what is most precious to me in this story is that when our scars are the most disfiguring, His eyes are tender toward us, overflowing with compassion. His touch is gentle. And He does not see ugliness in His children, but beauty.

DARK, YET LOVELY

"Dark am I, yet lovely..."
Song of Songs 1:5

The Surgeon surveyed the woman lying before Him.
Burned as a child, her every scar and blemish exposed beneath
His gaze.
A timid woman, long accustomed to hiding,
dares glance into His eyes.
Awaiting her glance, His tender eyes
overflowing with compassion
begin to wash away her fear.
Such gentleness, His fingers touch her cheeks,
her scars, her source of shame.
Knowing His plan, even now seeing her as she will be,
joyful with anticipation
He speaks with certain confidence,
"Oh, I see beauty here!"

"How can this be?" she wonders, "Dare I trust?"
Yet through that one glimpse into His eyes
she believes His Word;
She rests and submits to His work,
awaiting the day Heaven's curtain will be opened

and she will see her Savior face to face,
and see mirrored in His eyes the beauty she has longed for...
The gift of God, His righteousness.

Abba, what do You see when You look at me?
When the sins of my heart lay bare.
When there's no way to hide, no way to avoid
The depth of my need for a Savior.
Desperate for love, my hungry heart cries,
"What do You see, Abba?"
Your Word resounds—You see me washed clean,
Jesus in me,
You see me as I will be
Fully restored, my heart completely Yours.
God, please heal my deaf heart that deep inside
I may hear You whisper
These words of grace that are my life:
"Oh, I see beauty here!"

"You are altogether beautiful, my darling,
there is no flaw in you."
Song of Songs 4:7

"And we all, with unveiled face, continually
seeing as in a mirror the glory of the Lord,
are progressively being transformed into
His image from [one degree of] glory to
[even more] glory, which comes from the Lord,
[who is] the Spirit."
2 Corinthians 3:18 AMP

A Step Deeper In...

I invite you to take some time to honestly ask God, "Abba, what do you see when you look at me?" If you struggle to believe that He sees you as beautiful, ask Him to lead you to places in scripture that can replace the old lies you've believed with the truth.

Song of Songs is the place God speaks to me over and over about how He feels about me. This book is a love story poem about Jesus' love for us, His bride.

Over and over in this book, Jesus tells us we are beautiful and He is in love with us. He speaks it to each of us personally and individually. He knows your love language and He will answer your questions.

Just like He spoke to me through the TV, He sometimes speaks in unconventional ways. He can speak through people, circumstances, an inner knowing, a dream, a book or a magazine article among other things. However, His answer will never contradict scripture. Spending time reading God's written Word helps us recognize His voice when He speaks in unconventional ways.

Chapter 3

SPOKEN TO

IMAGINE YOURSELF SEATED shoulder to shoulder in a hot and crowded auditorium awaiting the address of the visiting evangelist, Dr. Billy Graham. Elderly now, this wise and respected man has come to your town by invitation to preach a message of hope.

No one knows that it was through this man's message years ago that you came to know Jesus Christ. You can still remember the words he spoke that day through the television set, powerful words that cut straight to your heart. The next day you wrote him a letter to thank him and sent him your picture. Now here he is, right before your eyes. As the applause dies down, this great man takes the microphone. "Ladies and gentlemen, before I begin I would like to speak a personal word to (your name), whom I recognize seated here in the front row. I just want to thank you for your letter and tell you that I have been praying for you all these years."

When someone I respect speaks to me, it communicates worth. The fact that he or she would notice me, remember my name, turn his or her attention to me and speak a kind word—this touches my core need to be valued.

When Jesus speaks to me, He is telling me that I am valuable to Him and He notices me. I've not yet heard Him speak audibly, but even the inaudible voice I hear through His Word or a thought or a song, when my spirit recognizes that it's the Lord, I am thrilled that the King of Kings would notice me and speak to me. This is the prayer I pray more than any other, "Jesus speak to me."

Jesus' words to me are gentle. They are soothing and comforting and tender like kisses. Romantic language is the language used in the Song of Songs. This is poetic, symbolic language. *"The kisses of His mouth" (Song of Songs 1:2)* is symbolic for the words He speaks to us that communicate His love. When I ask for His kisses I am asking Him to speak to me.

When Jesus speaks to believers, He is not harsh and condemning. That's how I tell the difference between His voice and the voice of the enemy.

When Satan throws out condemnation, it's like static on a cell phone, making it hard to hear Jesus. And it's often in the valleys that the static comes. At those times when it feels like I've lost connection with Jesus, I'm tempted to hang up and seek something else to touch that core hole deep within. But Jesus is not hanging up. He is right there on the other side of that static, calling my name and continuing to speak.

"Call to me and I will answer you and tell you great and unsearchable things you do not know." Isaiah 33:3

SPEAK TO ME

"Let him kiss me with the kisses of his mouth—
for your love is more delightful than wine."
Song of Songs 1:2

I miss You, my Master, Your kisses, my life.
The words of Your mouth like a sword or a knife
Cut to the depths of the thirst of my soul
Exciting, delighting me, filling the hole
That runs through my core
Unreached by mere wine,
Untouched by a table of pastries fine.
All this world offers me pales next to You.
I long for Your kisses, LORD, come speak anew.

A Step Deeper In...

My enemy, the devil, *"is a liar and the father of lies."* *(John 8:44)* He seeks to alienate me from God through deception. I think one of the chief lies he uses is the one that tells me God won't speak to me through the Bible. In my head, I know God speaks through the Bible, but to believe He will speak personally to me today is harder to hold onto.

This lie is what keeps people too busy to read God's Word. I know this is how it works for me. When I renounce that lie and believe the truth that God will speak personally to me through scripture, a hunger for the Word of God is awakened in me and those words on the page spring to life.

I challenge you today to ask God to speak to you through His word. Ask Him to help you replace this lie with truth. This can be a process. Search for scriptures that tell you God will speak to you and pray them before you read. Begin with Psalm 119, Hebrews 11:6 and Romans 10:17. Ask Him to lead you to others.

Chapter 4

DESIRED

Could God really desire *my* love? After all these years as a Christian, I am still tempted to believe the lie that what I have to give will not be precious to God. What is it about my love that He desires?

As I was returning home from a walk one day, with our property still far in the distance, I noticed something flapping around in the tall grass on the side of the road. Wondering what it could be, I continued plodding along. As I moved closer, my heart leapt to see that it was my children waving their arms.

Drawing nearer I realized they were jumping up and down waiting for me, excitement radiating out in all directions from their little bodies. They watched until finally I reached the edge of our property, and then they burst into a run toward me. I ran too, and scooped them up into my arms.

God spoke to me through my children. It had given me such joy to see them waiting for me, and He told me, "This is how I feel when I see My children waiting for Me, worshipping Me, hands raised, longing to see My face."

I am sure my children didn't comb their hair and change their clothes before they came out to the road that day. I don't remember—it didn't matter to me. What mattered was that they came because they wanted me—and it thrilled my soul!

This is the heart of worship.

One way we express worship to God is through singing. God tells us to sing to Him. *"Sing to the LORD a new song... For the LORD takes delight in his people..." (Psalm 149:1,4)* Singing to the LORD doesn't really accomplish anything or help anyone. It's different from other commands that He gives us: give to the poor, preach the Word, make disciples, carry each other's burdens. Of all the jobs we could do for Him, all the ways we could serve, here He's just wanting *us*. "Come sing to Me!"

I find it amazing that He asks us to do this for Him.

Singing to Him is offering ourselves to Him, open and vulnerable, and this delights Him! Just as the bride delights to hear Jesus speak in the Song of Songs, Jesus the Lover also delights to hear the bride speak to Him. He is thrilled with the bride's love. We can trust that when we offer our affection to Jesus through singing or whatever other forms we may use to express our love, He receives it as a treasure.

WORSHIP

"Let my beloved come into his garden and taste its choice fruits."
Song of Songs 4:16b

I am Your garden.
Come into me.
I want You to know me, and I want to know You.
Crush my fruit, release its flavor.
Let it be pure wine, nothing manmade.

"May the wine go straight to my beloved."

Come, pour out my soul and drink me in
And pour Your soul into me, making us one.
One taste of Your soul in mine and I am insatiable apart.
When Your silence surrounds me
My emptiness echoes, aching to taste You again.

"His mouth is sweetness itself; he is altogether lovely.
This is my beloved, this is my friend..."

Come rest in my garden.
Lay Your hands on my heart.
Draw out all the fragrant colors of a life laid down.
Evergreen passionate worship
That will not be quenched or turn brown.
When You hold back the rain, make me strong.
Lead my roots to the streams that flow unseen
Deep in Your love that supports me.

You are my Gardener.
When You come into me, I come alive.
I yearn to feel You walk through me,
Creating by Your touch and breath every leaf and fruit.
Come pull the weeds. Leave no corner untouched.
I want to be beautiful for You.

"...my own vineyard is mine to give..."

And I give it to You, Jesus.

Song of Songs 5:16, 7:9 and 8:12

A Step Deeper In...

The most painful things in my life have involved unveiling my heart to someone and then being rejected. Thus, opening up my heart sometimes feels like the time when, as part of a wilderness youth group outing, I tried to get myself to jump off a 30-foot cliff into a Colorado river. I desperately wanted to jump, but I also felt like throwing up.

Stand today on the edge of that 30-foot cliff. Look down at the rushing river of God's love and believe that He is safe, and He *desires* you. Go ahead... jump.

Open your heart and pour out your love to Him like a child. One of my five children hugs me tightly and long and gazes into my eyes. One kisses me straight on the lips quickly and then giggles. One draws me a picture. One invites me to spend time together. One smiles and puts his arm around me. Each child's love is just as precious to me and if they hold back, I feel the loss. Only that child can give the love I desire deeply. Write a poem or a love letter, sing a song, dance, create something like a picture, give an extravagant gift... just do it all for Him.

Take time to meditate on these verses...

"How delightful is your love, my sister, my bride!
How much more pleasing is your love than wine
and the fragrance of your perfume more than any spice!
Your lips drop sweetness as the honeycomb, my bride;
milk and honey are under your tongue."
Song of Songs 4:10,11a

"Open to me... my dove..."
Song of Songs 5:2

Chapter 5

HEARD

GOD WANTS TO HEAR our voices in worship, but He also wants us to pour out our sorrows to Him. At times, I have poured out my heart to someone only to have them respond in such a way that I knew they hadn't really heard. They didn't hear the pain, the core of my heart. They responded to something else, but they never truly understood. They only magnified my loneliness.

At the core of the Gospel is the truth that God *heard*. All the grief, all the sorrow, all the loneliness and pain that sin has brought into our lives since conception, every time we have cried or tried to explain it to someone else and they've missed it - Jesus heard.

I do not think it was a coincidence that when Jesus first entered Jerusalem as a newborn baby, at the start of the New Testament gospel of Jesus Christ, the first person to recognize Jesus and announce His arrival was an old man named Simeon. The name "Simeon" means "God heard." Sometimes before we can receive the solution to our pain, we need to know we've been heard.

Our Creator knows this about us. And He wants us to know that when He hears, He acts. He came to be our Savior.

In Luke 2, we are told so little of Simeon's life. The details are left to our imagination. All we know for sure is that he was waiting for Jesus, waiting intensely. He believed God and trusted in His goodness that He would indeed come to comfort His people.

When I became pregnant with our fifth child I was going through a time of grief. Among a string of losses, I found myself in the middle of an excruciatingly difficult church split. My dearest friends left the church and the spiritual and emotional safety in which I had flourished disintegrated. Distrust ruled, and I could share little of my grief with anyone.

In the midst of this darkness God surprisingly blessed us with a baby boy, after I had lost all hope of ever having another baby. In this one gift God spoke mountains of love to me. I knew that He had heard my grief and sent me comfort. When we heard the name "Simeon" and learned it meant "God heard" we knew this was the name we wanted for our baby. His life would be a testimony of God's faithfulness.

THE WATCHMAN'S SHOUT OF JOY

Luke 2:25-35

A lifetime of watching people suffer, uncomforted.
Hard labor, poverty, pain, disease, death, slavery, sorrow.
Simeon...year after year obedience... faithfully following.
Waiting...waiting a lifetime for one glimpse of the Comforter.

Searching the scriptures.
Over and over, God promised a Savior, a Comforter.
Crying out. A lifetime of crying to see God's face.
A cry so deep in his bones that they nearly broke in the yearning.
He had to see Jesus.

Many times he almost lost hope
As he watched some disease or tragedy sweep through his village,
Raping the people he loved, with no mercy.
But something stronger than himself kept him holding on,
Kept him connected to that cord of hope:

"The LORD will surely comfort Zion..." Isaiah 51:3

Hadn't this been impressed on him all his life?
It was his name.
Every time he was called, the reminder came...*"God Heard."*
His mother had told him her grief,
God heard and answered.
And she believed and passed this to him,
To be woven into the core of who he was.

A lifetime of seeing suffering could not change his name.
Every cell in his being knew that the Comforter would come
And he would see his face.
Simeon came to proclaim
That though the way is long and the suffering great...

God Heard

And He has given us Jesus.
In one glimpse we find peace, and in joy let go of the world.

"Listen! Your watchmen lift up their voices;
together they shout for joy.
When the LORD returns to Zion,
they will see it with their own eyes.
Burst into songs of joy together,
you ruins of Jerusalem,
for the LORD has comforted his people,
he has redeemed Jerusalem."
Isaiah 52:8,9

A Step Deeper In...

Have you ever really poured your heart out to the LORD as you would to a close friend? I mean, like go into all the gory details? Tell Him the whole story. Yes, He already knows, but He still wants you to tell Him because He wants to listen to you.

At times, I have known of a weight my child was carrying. I knew already what had happened. But I wanted him to tell me all about it because then I could help him carry it. I could hear him, and he would feel comforted and not alone. We would share intimacy.

I have found that it is easier for me to pour out my heart to the LORD if I do it while out for a walk. I like the privacy of a country road rather than a populated subdivision, because sometimes I cry and sometimes I need to be loud. If I'm inside, I kneel at a table and imagine the LORD in the chair beside me.

What situations help you pour out your heart to a friend? Create such a situation with the LORD. Maybe that will mean a walk on a country road, or a cup of tea and an empty chair across the table, or maybe you talk best while you're running or working at some mindless task. Whatever helps you open up to a friend, try doing it while you imagine the LORD there listening. Because He is, and He hears you. And when He hears, He acts.

Chapter 6

CHOSEN

To THE BEST OF MY recollection, this is how it happened. The bell rang, and we were out the door in a flash headed for the soccer field. The two best players at Glenn Loomis Elementary School took their places as team captains and the rest of us lined up in a semi-circle around them.

It was just like any other recess. We would quickly pick teams and then play as hard and long as we could until the bell rang again. I was never the first one picked, but I had performed exceptionally well at the last recess. I loved the game and was anxious to get started. And then it happened...David, the biggest, strongest, most respected captain of the school chose first, and to the astonishment of many—he chose me! I imagine that many jaws fell that day as I rose, glowing, to take my place of honor beside the captain.

Being chosen...what is more honoring than this? *"You did not choose me, but I chose you..." John 15:16*

"God has chosen you from the beginning for salvation..."
2 Thessalonians 2:13 AMP

"Therefore, as God's chosen people, holy and dearly loved..."
Colossians 3:12

In passage after passage, God shouts to us, *"You* are the one I want!"

God has given us marriage and adoption to represent the relationship He longs for with us; both revolve around being chosen. A man and woman choose each other to be husband and wife. Together they might choose to adopt a child, one they love even before she becomes theirs.

From the beginning of time, God chose specific people for specific positions and tasks. But unlike my experience of being chosen for the soccer team, His choices are not performance-based. *"Brothers, think of what you were when you were called... But God chose the foolish things of the world to shame the wise; God chose the weak things of the world to shame the strong. God chose the lowly things of this world and the despised things...so that no one may boast before Him." 1 Corinthians 1:27-29*

God chose a tiny, no-name, stiff-necked people to become Israel, His "chosen people." He chose the disciples individually, one by one, ordinary sinful men with pride and selfishness, to be his friends; to have them at his side for His entire ministry.

I think I would have chosen to maybe live down the street from them, where I could teach them and minister to them, but then be able to get away to my own space. But Jesus didn't do that. He would sneak away at night sometimes to pray, but He chose to be with them always. He actually wanted to be with them. He loved them. He enjoyed them.

I am not usually chosen by people. I easily blend into the background, unnoticed and insignificant. I'm quiet and don't have a loud, funny, charismatic personality. Much of the time I can't think of anything to say. The amazing truth that Jesus has chosen me thrills me. I pray that as you read the following poem and meditate on the scriptures, Jesus will capture your heart afresh with the truth that the one He wants, the one He's chosen, is you!

UNDER HIS GRACE

Luke 5:1-11

A common fisherman, nothing more.
Laboring long, far off shore.
Nothing to show at the end of the day
A weary heart, longing to lay
Down this fruitless way of life
Ridden with loneliness, striving and strife.

Then Jesus spoke to me, "May I come in?
I'll rest in your vessel and bear your sin."
Something about this Man gave me hope.
I willingly, eagerly gave Him my boat.
But then He asked of me one thing more—
"Trust Me and row out again far from shore."

That was how He uncovered my need.
"I can't do that," I began to plead.
"I've tried it before with no success.
I just don't have what it takes, I guess."
But his eyes encouraged me, "Try again."
"I will, my Lord." I said with a grin,
Trying to cover the fear within.

"What is it this man sees in me?"
I thought as I drifted out to sea.
"What is it about Him? It's something deep—
Wild and untamed like the waves beneath...
Billowing strength, a mystery to me...
Calling me, wooing me, who can He be?
I want to be with Him, that's all I know,"
I thought as I grasped the oars to row.

Dropping my nets, I waited with doubt
But what I saw then made me rise up and shout
"Oh, my Lord, what have You done?!
Just look at them filling my nets one by one!"

Flopping fish squirmed about
Amidst my own astonished shouts
Like water sprayed into my face
The mist off God's strong sea of grace.
Like the taste of salt that filled the air
I could not grasp what I knew was there—
The power of God for all to see.
Who is this Man who's chosen me?

I fell down at His knees and cried,
"My sin, my selfishness, my pride...
Leave me, Lord, I cannot stand
Beneath the power of Your command."

But then He spoke to me, "Don't be afraid."
Billowing mercy I found in His gaze.
As wild as His strength, this love captured me.
A captive, and yet finally free
To leave behind all that I've known
And follow God for He has shown
His power to take my barren life
And from His harvest fields of white
Draw men to me that need to see
His mercy and His majesty.

The testimony of my life
Will be that Christ has paid the price
And He is worthy of all praise
My life I'll live under His grace.

A Step Deeper In...

When I read a verse of scripture it may resonate as truth to me, but it doesn't roar with power in my heart until I spend time meditating on it, rolling it over and over in my mind, praying for more revelation and faith to believe it. The verses in this chapter are ones that can roar with power within you to bring strength when you feel weak. Take time to meditate on them this week and relax into the amazing grace of being chosen.

Chapter 7

KNOWN

WHEN I WAS A TEENAGER, and into my twenties, I was bulimic. A few people eventually knew, but for the most part I lived a desperately lonely, secret life. My days revolved around trying to control my eating and my weight. I was a slave to bingeing and purging and the self-hatred that fueled it all. My heart was full of unforgiveness, fear and suicidal depression.

I felt like I walked around in a glass box, able to see the people around me, but unable to feel their touch and receive their love. They offered me love, which I outwardly accepted, but in my heart, I rejected it thinking "If you only knew the ugly thoughts I have, you wouldn't love me." My soul was starving because I wouldn't take in love from people who didn't really know me, which was everyone. And shame kept me hiding.

I can relate to the woman at the well in John 4. In this chapter John describes an encounter of Jesus with a woman as He sat down to rest beside a well, about noon one day.

Women normally came to draw water together in the cooler morning or evening hours, but this woman came alone, at noon, when no one else would be there to ridicule her shame. She had been married five times and was currently living with a man outside of marriage.

In a culture where women were stoned for committing adultery, this woman lived under a crushing weight of rejection. But Jesus compassionately reached out to her, asking for a drink. As their conversation unfolded, He revealed to her that He already knew her secrets, her sin and her shame. And yet rather than rejecting her, He had come to be her Savior.

Though, unlike this woman, my shame was hidden from public view, it still prevented me from receiving the love of people and of God. And shame can still send me running for cover. Yet Jesus has a way of tenderly pulling back the curtain that I'm hiding behind, but then looking me in the eye with a warm smile that says "I died for you. That sin is paid. You are Mine! I see you and I know you and I love you!"

LIVING WATER

Just another day.
I lifted my jar and walked to the well.
The people parted as I passed.
Occasionally I caught a glance,
But mostly they just looked away.
The whole town knew what I had done.
They knew my life, what I'd become.
But no one knew my heart...
Until that day.

Waiting there when I arrived
He warmly looked me in the eyes.
Not a look like others gave,
But humbly open, as if to say
"Come on in!"

I thought it strange that He was there
And stranger yet that He would care
To talk with me...a stranger.
He seemed to know me from the start—
I mean He truly knew my heart.
I wish I could describe to you His eyes.
Love is all that I can say.
He looked at me with
love that day.

At first, I thought it was because
He didn't know who I was.
He smiled and asked me for a drink.
And then He told me what I think
I've searched for all my life.

He said He'd give me water
That would fill the ache inside.
That hungry, thirsty spot deep down
that I could never satisfy.
The spot I tried to fill with men
Only to be hurt again.

He told me all about me, everything I'd done.
He knew my sin completely, and yet
He was Someone
Unlike any other man I know.
He didn't leave. He didn't go.
My sin was out, fully exposed,
and yet His tender gaze...
He washed me.
My shame completely fell away.
And when He told me who He was
I dropped my jar right there.

Jesus Christ is God Himself!
I could only stand and stare
In awe, soak in this mystery.
Jesus the Living Water, here to set me free!

"Come, see a man who told me everything
I ever did..."

And loved me!

John 4

A Step Deeper In...

Like me, you might have heard this story (John 4) a million times already. Pray that Jesus will speak to you afresh through it. Ask Him to pull back the curtain that you hide behind and let you see His tender eyes.

Chapter 8

SEEN

Seen. There is something very deep about that word. One time in our city a reporter published an article in our local newspaper about a Christian worship meeting. Along with the article, he included a photograph of the crowd of worshippers, taken from the front of the meeting, looking right into their faces. What stood out to me was the photo. The entire crowd of worshippers were blurred out around one lone worshipper who was solely in focus. This is what it means to be "seen" by God. When we come before Him in worship, His eyes are fixed on each one of us as if you or I are the only one in the room with Him.

As we walk through our lives with Him, amidst the crowds and chaos that often surrounds us, we have this same depth of attention. He "sees" us.

One day, as Jesus was about to enter the town of Nain, he was met by a funeral procession just passing out through the gate.

The procession was led by a widow grieving the loss of her only son. *"When the Lord saw her, his heart went out to her..." Luke 7:13*

Jesus not only noticed her, but when he saw her, He *knew her.* He knew what she was feeling. He knew her pain. And He loved her. We can be seen in a way that brings judgment and shame. But when Jesus saw this mother, "His heart went out to her."

When I read this story, I began to pray for deeper revelation on this. "Jesus, what did You feel for her? Please show me what it was like for You when Your heart went out to her."

A large part of the glory of God is wrapped up in His emotions, particularly what He feels for us when He sees us in our pain and sin and brokenness. We do not have an emotionless Savior. *"Jesus Christ is the same yesterday and today and forever"* (Hebrews 13:8) and whatever He felt for that woman He must also feel for us when our hearts are broken.

WHEN THE LORD SAW HER

"When the Lord saw her, his heart went out to her...
Then he went up and touched the bier...
and Jesus gave him back to his mother."
Luke 7:11-17

I saw a woman, my daughter, my bride.
Her heart now lay broken, all mangled inside.
This heart I had formed with My own hands,
Tenderly, carefully, just as I planned.
I had filled it with love so deep for her boy,
A drop of My own love laden with joy.
Now here she wept, her heart in such pain.
How could I bear to stand back and abstain
From giving the life I was sent here to give.
"Father, may I let him live?"

Her grief overwhelmed me. I had to step out.
My anger consumed me I wanted to shout
"This should not be! Not this one that I love!
Not my daughter, my bride, my sister, my dove."
I could hardly bear the pain in her eyes
It was like a sword had pierced the skies
Thrust hard into the depths of my soul
And left me there with a gaping hole.
Time after time I had felt this before.
Countless women, those I adored
Watching them walk this march of grief
After cleaving to Me with relentless belief
Crying out for Me to hear
And make known the truth that I am near.

It was then the dam broke.
All these years I'd held back.
My love, a torrent burst through the gap.
"Father, yes, this is the time
To let my bride know she is Mine.
And I have come to set her free
To show for all eternity
Her son will live and so will she."
Just one touch, but clearly a sign
That I've not ignored these ones that are mine.
For to each woman deep in grief my love
begs to be released.
And I've come to touch her loved one too
And say, "My child, be made new!"
The time will come, indeed it is near
When I will take this child so dear
And healed, restored and fully alive
Give him back to his mother, never to die.

A Step Deeper In...

There are treasures hidden in the secret caverns of God's Word, waiting to be discovered. Dive deep into one story of an incident in Jesus' life, such as the one this poem is based on. Ask God to lead you to a secret cavern where He has hidden a treasure.

As you study, ask Him questions about His emotions. "LORD, what were you feeling when you saw that person? LORD, what did you feel when you walked into that place?"

Chapter 9

VALUED

I BEGAN PARENTHOOD with lofty dreams of raising godly, happy, emotionally healthy, issue-less kids. They would be missionaries who would give their lives to Jesus and serve Him free of the baggage and struggles I entered adulthood with. I devoured parenting books, magazines, videos and conferences that would help me to be the best mom I could be to my precious innocent little ones.

But as my five beautiful children grew and gradually became teenagers, the heavy weight of realization crushed in on me that I had failed in many ways to meet their needs. My children were going through some major struggles that I had contributed to, and that I could not fix. Could God be pleased with me now?

I thoroughly believed that parenting my children was the main job God had called me to. I was a full-time homemaker and a home-schooling mom and I had given my all to follow Jesus by being the best wife and mom I could. But now FAILURE was stamped in big black letters across the envelope that held my job description.

What does God think of us when we fail? Maybe an even better question is... "What does He see as success?" One night a sudden realization came to me—what God wants from us is... relationship.

That's it. That is what He's after; that's His goal. That's what gives Him pleasure. What He wants from us is that we would turn toward Him, come to Him, trust Him. There are things He wants us to do as we follow Him, but He doesn't need us to do a job for Him. If we fail at a job, He's not disgusted. He sees it as an opportunity to draw us into a deeper relationship of trust in Him.

Jesus can handle my children's struggles. He died to wash away all their sin and pain and be their Savior. He alone will complete the good work He's begun in each of them. And as for me, He paints that envelope with white-out and labels it in big, bold, red permanent marker letters "SUCCESS," because He looks at my heart, clean through Jesus' blood, and He values my weak, imperfect love for Him above everything. To Him, it's all about relationship.

If you have known major failure and especially public failure, then you know what it's like to be judged by people who peer in the windows but don't want to enter the room and meet you there in all your raw pain. Jesus does. *"The LORD is close to the brokenhearted..." Psalm 34:18*

When I am brokenhearted I am not always easy to be with. Sometimes I am angry; sometimes I am filled with doubts about God's goodness. Whatever I may be feeling at those times I can rest assured that Jesus won't be pushed away. In the face of my deepest failures, the good news of the gospel is that in Christ I am valued, not for what I do, but for who I am—His.

And He will never let go of my hand.

GRACE

"His pleasure is not in the strength of the horse, nor his delight in the legs of the warrior; the LORD delights in those who fear him, who put their hope in his unfailing love."
Psalm 147:10,11

"When my heart was grieved and my spirit embittered, I was senseless and ignorant; I was a brute beast before you. Yet I am always with you; you hold me by my right hand."
Psalm 73:21-23

A pitcher of milk held tightly with care,
Small chubby hands and brown curly hair,
A little red dress and black patent shoes,
A shiny clean kitchen and dishes brand new.
I want to please Mama and do it just right.
Setting the table is my job tonight.

I don't really know how it happened.
Somehow my foot caught the door.
Shattered and splattered, a milk and glass mixture
Now covers the kitchen floor.
And now here I lie in a puddle,
A mess and a broken heart.
I wanted so badly to please my Mama
And do it all right from the start.

Oh no, here she comes! What will she think
When she sees this mess on the floor?
The meal is all ruined and company's coming.
I hear them now at the door.

I run to get towels and work really hard
To try my best to undo.
But the damage is done and this spilled milk
I can never make brand new.
The tears stream down and I hide my face
As Mama walks in the room.
"I'm so sorry Mom. I made a mess.
Now what do I do?"
But to my surprise, with tender eyes
She asks, "Child, how are you?
There's glass in your hands and your dress is ripped
And that bruise must have come
When somehow you slipped.
I can clean up this mess and the people can wait.
It's you, Precious Child, my heart breaks ...For you."

That was a long, long time ago; I lived to please
my mom.
But now I live to please the LORD.
His delight in me is my reward.
My job is bigger now. The mess I've made now greater.
Splattered relationships, shattered trust—
And it's getting later and later.
I've worked really hard to clean it up
And put it all back together,
But it seems all I've done is smear it around
And the mess has grown even bigger.
Oh, no! Here He comes! What does He think
As He sees me here on my face?
All I want is to know His love and hide in His embrace.
Judging eyes peer in the windows
But they don't knock on the door.

They don't know what to say, I guess
When they see the messy floor.
But Jesus walks right by them, throws open the door,
Pulls down every shade and meets me there on the floor.
"Oh, My Child, I understand. I know you did your best.
Let Me hold you for awhile, then we'll clean the mess.
Show me where your heart is breaking.
Let Me see the cuts.
It's you I care about right now.
Please... open your heart up."

A Step Deeper In...

As you look back over your life, ask God what He thinks when He looks at your past. Ask Him to lead you to scriptures that confirm the answer He gave you. His whispers will never contradict His written word.

Chapter 10

OPENED

THERE ARE MANY ACCOUNTS recorded for us in the Bible of people Jesus healed. Among them are the blind, the deaf, the lame, the demon-possessed, and even the dead, raised to life again. Sometimes I read these stories over quickly with little emotion, little true awe overwhelming my heart. I've heard them before. I read them quickly without imagining the amazing wonder of each moment described. I have to slow myself down. I pray that Jesus will help me enter into what that person experienced of Him that I have not yet.

In Mark 7:32-35 we are told of a man who was brought to Jesus because he was deaf and had a speech impediment. Those who brought him begged Jesus to lay His hands on him, hoping this would bring healing.

In these few short verses we are told how Jesus took the man aside, away from the crowd, and performed a miracle. Jesus put His fingers in the man's ears. He touched the man's tongue with

His own saliva. He stood before him skin to skin, face to face. This was not a miracle Jesus wanted to do from a distance, and not in the chaos of a crowd. No — Jesus knew the loneliness that this man had lived with.

Can you imagine the isolation that this man knew? Year after year being unable to speak to anyone...all his thoughts, dreams, fears bottled up inside. He could see people around him laughing together, whispering secrets, shouting, singing...while his questions remained unasked, his secrets unshared, his soul locked up in silent darkness.

Jesus could have just spoken the word and the man would have been healed. But Jesus gave him not only physical healing, but also the deep relational connection he longed for. And that healing opened up, not only his relationship with Jesus, but it also opened up his ability to now know and be known by others.

As I took time to meditate on the words of this story, God began to soften the callousness of my familiarity with the text. God's grace expressed through this act of kindness to one needy man in history, is also extended to me. In fact, it is offered to us all.

We each need Jesus to open up our spiritual hearing, in order for us to be able to communicate with Him. And that is what He is eager to do.

When one becomes a Christian, Jesus personally opens up our capacity to hear His voice. He gives us the ability to know Him and this becomes the foundation from which we can also know and be truly known by others. However, the fullness of our healing is yet to come.

I remember many nights lying in bed as a child, tormented with fear, trying to talk with my Dad-- the one I trusted most-- about what was troubling me. I made him turn out the light so he wouldn't see my face. And my few words came out haltingly and with excruciating difficulty. I was closed.

When I think back to those lonely years I realize with gratefulness how much Jesus has opened me. And yet, despite the richness of relationship I now enjoy with God, my family and my friends, I have a longing for intimacy that remains significantly unsatisfied. I experience scattered moments of transparent connection with people, but most of my days are lived out with some measure of loneliness. When I speak, I often feel like there is more in my soul than I can pull out and put into words. When I listen to others speak, I feel restless to move beneath the surface chitchat. I experience an intimate relationship with God, but I still have to sift through a great fog of cloudiness.

"For now we see in a mirror dimly, but then face to face. Now I know in part; then I shall know fully, even as I am fully known." 1 Corinthians 13:12 ESV

Beyond the Christian's initial opening in this life, there is a much fuller experience of being opened that awaits us when we see Jesus face to face.

It's like there is a floodgate, and right now a strong trickle seeps through. But one day soon Jesus will again cry out "BE OPENED!" And then... we can only imagine what it will be like to open up to the shameless freedom of relationship that God has designed us for.

"Ephphatha!"

"After he took him aside, away from the crowd, Jesus put his fingers
into the man's ears. Then he spit and touched the man's tongue.
He looked up to heaven and with a deep sigh said to him,
"Ephphatha!" (which means, "Be opened!"). At this, the man's ears
were opened, his tongue was loosened and he began to speak plainly."
Mark 7:33-35

The loneliness, it closes in
Once again...is it my sin?
Is it my fault I cannot hear
Your voice that whispers in my ear?
Take me aside. Draw me and hide
My face from those who criticize
My awkward way of speaking words
The fear that leaves your words unheard.
Open me! Oh LORD, I cry!
Desperate screams in silence lie
Buried deep within this cell
Below what even I could tell
If I could speak as a free man.
I want to know you, Son of Man.
Put Your fingers in my ears.
Your clear voice I long to hear.
Let water from Your mouth touch mine
That I can speak by Your design.
Unleash Your deep compassion's sigh
A wordless groan sighs through your eyes.
Words of life flow free—no fear.
Unbound, untied, no compromise...
Focused on my Father's eyes...free!

A Step Deeper In...

Do the words of this poem resonate in your own heart? Do you long to know Jesus more? Tell Him what you want. Let that buried cry rise to the surface.

Chapter 11

HEALED

For most of my life I have tended toward emotional dependency— the idolatry of letting a person take God's place in my life, looking to him or her to tell me who I am and provide the comfort and security I need. For some people, rather than depending on a person, they lean on a job or a toy or a hobby. It's part of our fallen human condition, and the obstacle that blocks our path to knowing God. Our lives are a journey of learning to place our trust in Christ alone.

Healing, both physical and emotional, was part of the package when we received the gospel of God's grace. Though our healing will not be complete until we see Jesus face to face, we have received significant ongoing healing in this life.

Sometimes God heals a broken place in us through some touch of another believer. When that happens, it can be tempting to put our trust more in that person than in Jesus Himself. But Jesus wants us to know that the healing He offers us is rooted in His

Name, in Who He is — our Savior who died for us and purchased us with His blood. When He gives us His Name to hold onto, our healing is secure, irrevocable, permanent, *ours*.

I came to Jesus nameless, just one insignificant person among the millions of people on earth, a cripple, in need of miraculous inner healing. I spent my days searching for The Healer. In Bible times those who were crippled couldn't enter the temple. So too my brokenness brought shame, preventing me from entering in to receive God's love.

But the good news is that God desired to heal me! And when I simply put my trust in Jesus to forgive my sins and make me His child, He gave me His Name. I was adopted, and I became like a new bride who received her husband's name and immediately became a co-heir of His inheritance. Everything contained in that name was suddenly mine.

The day I married I became Susan Popa. I remember how awkward it felt and how unnatural it was to sign my name. If someone called me by my new name it didn't feel like me. This is how it was when Jesus gave me His Name. I am gradually growing to trust that His Name is really mine.

Now when I approach God, it's like I come as a daughter-in-law, Susan Jesus. I've received the family name. I've been forever sealed *"into an inheritance that can never perish, spoil or fade."* (1 Peter 1:4) And that inheritance includes the complete restoration and healing of my spirit, soul and body.

If a man was to give his wife the extravagant gift of a tropical island vacation, he might say... "This is the flight number. Don't worry, I've reserved it for you in my name. And there's a luxury suite reserved for you when you get there — it's in my name. And each night you can dine at the finest restaurant. I've reserved the best seat there for you, overlooking the ocean — it's reserved for you in my name." I think this is what Jesus has done for me by giving me His Name.

Do we need peace? He has purchased it and reserved it for us in His Name, which is now ours. Do we need joy, or deliverance, or healing, or freedom from shame? It is reserved for us in Jesus' Name — which is now ours. When we know what Christ purchased for us on the cross, and that He has given us complete access to it all through His Name, we can be fearless in approaching the Father to ask for what we need. *"...your name is like perfume poured out."* *(Song of Songs 1:3)* When I approach God as a daughter-in-law, having received the family name, whoever I was before is now smothered with the overwhelming unspeakably beautiful fragrance of the poured-out perfume of Jesus' Name.

Lovely perfume is something that we cannot even find words to describe. It just pervades the whole atmosphere and speaks beauty that we cannot define.

"But thanks be to God, who in Christ always leads us in triumphal procession, and through us spreads the fragrance of the knowledge of him everywhere. For we are the aroma of Christ to God among those who are being saved and among those who are perishing." 2 Corinthians 2:14,15 ESV

THE NAME OF JESUS

A nameless beggar – a cripple since birth
Forty years searching for someone on earth
To heal the broken place inside
That brought such shame and made him hide
His face from the crowd that passed him by
As they entered the temple of God most High.

His hand outstretched, but eyes cast down
When suddenly he heard the sound
Of men of God who spoke with power
Because their eyes saw God's desire
To raise him from this mud and mire.

Mercy gazing into his eyes
Seeing past every fear and disguise
They gently took him by the hand
And then... they helped him stand!
New life burst forth within his bones
Walls of self-hatred now crumbled stones
For HE WAS FREE!
Entering the temple now
He clings to the men who showed him how
To walk and run and dance and leap;
If he lets them go, will this healing keep?
But again, God speaks, "They are nameless, like you.
It is Jesus' Name, hold to Him, He holds you."

As these words hit their mark
Peace pierced through his heart
He finally could relax his hold
And stand upright before the Lord.

His strength and healing rooted deep
In something he could always keep....
The Name of Jesus.

"While the man held on to Peter and John,
all the people were astonished and came running to them...
When Peter saw this, he said to them:
'Fellow Israelites, why does this surprise you?
Why do you stare at us as if by our own power or godliness
we had made this man walk?... By faith in the name of Jesus,
this man whom you see and know was made strong.'"
Acts 3:11-16

A Step Deeper In

Take a moment to stop and imagine the poured-out perfume of Jesus' Name. This, our gift from Him, has the power and authority to overcome every stench of death or disease or trouble we face. Where in your life do you need the fragrance of the name of Jesus? It is yours! Speak it lavishly!

Chapter 12

FREED

I DON'T WANT TO GIVE the impression that just because we now have Jesus' name everything will be instantly and effortlessly placed in our laps. Scripture shows us that "entering the Promised Land" of freedom happens instantaneously on one level but is also taken battle by battle on another level.

In the Old Testament when the Israelites were set free from slavery in Egypt they had to leave their homes behind and walk on out. Yes, God parted the sea, but they had to walk or run straight through the middle despite their fears and the terrifying sounds of their slave drivers pursuing them. They reached the other side collapsing exhausted, and utterly spent, though also exhilarated to experience such a grand deliverance.

In the New Testament Paul says, *"...I press on to take hold of that for which Christ Jesus took hold of me. Brothers and sisters, I do not consider myself yet to have taken hold of it. But one thing I do: Forgetting what is behind and straining toward what is ahead, I press on toward the goal to win the prize for which God has called me heavenward in Christ Jesus." Philippians 3:12-14*

The good news of the gospel is that Jesus has set us free from sin, and He's parted the waters before us. But we need to walk into that freedom. When we repeatedly turn to anything besides Jesus to meet the needs of our hearts, that thing we turn to becomes a chain of bondage.

A chain could be food, alcohol, drugs, lying, stealing, any sin or relationship we turn to for the satisfaction our souls seek; satisfaction that can truly only be met in Christ.

Only Christ can meet our needs for unfailing love, peace, joy, security, identity, comfort, strength, etc. Leanne Payne, in her wonderful book, *The Healing Presence,* says on page 59:

"Spiritually and psychologically, to use C.S. Lewis' telling image of fallen man, man is "bent". The *unfallen* position was, as it were, a *vertical* one, one of standing erect, face turned upward to God in a listening-speaking relationship. It was a position of receiving continually one's true identity from God.

But fallen man is bent toward the creature and trapped in the continual attempt to find his identity in the created rather than in the Uncreated." She also says on page 60:

"The key to healing these bent ones is simple but profound, and the same for all: It consists in renouncing and utterly forsaking the "bent" posture toward the creature, and "straightening up" into Christ. There, standing upright in the vertical position, fully focused on God, our bonds from the old bent position fall off... It is the free state of listening-obedience where we find healing, completion and our true identity." (*The Healing Presence,* Baker Book House Company, 1995, pp. 59, 60)

We are like flowers that need to look toward the sun, their source of nourishment. If we think a person or thing is what will satisfy our souls, we become bent toward that person or thing, and it becomes our idol. Our healing comes when we learn to stop looking to that person or thing to tell us who we are, and to look instead to Jesus. We must straighten up into the Son and find our true identity in Christ alone. That healing that allows us to let go of the chains and straighten up into the Son is often a process.

I received some deep inner healing through working with a counselor. God was the source of this healing, but it flowed through her in many ways. It was hard for me to let her go, but this relationship was a chain that God wanted me free from.

God was so tender with me, graciously helping me separate from her. He didn't just yank her away, but gently helped me learn to straighten up into Him and hear Him tell me who I am, so that I was healed inside before I needed to completely let her go.

There is a phenomenon in nature that demonstrates how God helps us let go of the chains that once helped us cope with life, but that we must leave behind to be free. As a snake grows, God forms brand-new beautiful scales beneath the old skin. He works a miracle to allow that snake to separate from something it was once totally dependent on.

When we yield up our idols to God, knowing how entrenched we are in these attachments, He can work a miracle in our hearts that allows us to fully let them go.

When a snake is ready to shed the old skin, he cannot just take it off by himself. He has to lean into a rock. As he presses hard into the rock the skin is shed. We also cannot shed our idols by mere willpower. It is only as we learn to lean on Jesus, pressing hard into our Rock, that we can let them go.

The process of letting go of my counselor was hard work. But the work was not that of will-power, but of pressing hard into Jesus. As thoughts of her came, I learned to release them up to God in faith that she is not my security, but God's love is. I would lay the longing ache before Him and pray "Abba, please heal me. Please fill this void with new expressions of your love for me." As God answered that prayer over and over, my faith grew. Healing came like the layers of new flesh filling in a deep wound. When a wound undergoes debridement, the scabs are pulled back so that the new flesh can fill in the hole. Each time the wound was reopened like this I would run to Him as my Abba, my Papa, and I would ask Him, "How do you feel about me right now?" I worked hard at quieting my heart to listen and hear His whispers.

Idols are maintained with lies that we believe. We must pray for God to expose the lies we're believing, and make His truth known to us. My main prayer these last years has been "God, I want to know You." I pray that constantly, because the more He reveals Himself to me the more I fall in love with Him. When I catch a glimpse of Jesus and one taste of His love for me, the idols in my life crumble.

"By faith Moses, when he had grown up, refused to be known as the son of Pharaoh's daughter. He chose to be mistreated along with the people of God rather than to enjoy the fleeting pleasures of sin. He regarded disgrace for the sake of Christ as of greater value than the treasures of Egypt, because he was looking ahead to his reward. By faith he left Egypt, not fearing the king's anger; he persevered because he saw Him who is invisible." Hebrews 11:24-27

LEANING INTO THE ROCK

"And I will ask the Father,
and He will give you another Helper
(Comforter, Advocate, Intercessor—
Counselor, Strengthener, Standby)
to be with you forever—the Spirit of truth..."
John 14:16,17 AMP

A chance meeting, as people would say.
It had been a year, almost to the day.
Long enough to separate, but not quite to let go.
A counselor, but more than that.
God's love she helped me know.
There she was, suddenly before me.
Instinctively, I called her name.
Would this one I loved remember?
It was only a moment, yet I saw in her eyes
The love once there was gone.
And yet a bigger truth prevailed...
My need was also gone.
I've grown!
Newborn colors alive with boldness and intricate design,
The fresh scales of a brand-new creation
Lie just below the surface of an old covering.

Leaning into the Rock, the skin is shed.
What once covered me — touching, protecting, holding the new
life that formed within —
Now lies separate, faded, no longer needed.
And my Creator says, "Walk on, Child, walk on."

A Step Deeper In...

Is there anything in your life that you find yourself turning to repeatedly to meet the needs of your heart... to meet the needs that can only be truly met in Jesus? Why not take some time to pray and bring this question to the LORD?

Lean into Jesus and ask Him to help you shed this old skin. Refuse to continue turning to it, and instead ask Him to fill that void with new expressions of His love for you. Pray that God will expose the lies you've believed that keep you running to that idol.

Chapter 13

NOT ABANDONED

THE PAIN OF ABANDONMENT can be devastating; to watch the one who could meet your deepest needs turn and walk away, leaving you unprovided for, unprotected and unloved. There have been times I have felt abandoned by God. I have read the scriptures that show His power to heal and do miracles, and those that promise that He hears my every prayer and can meet my every need. I believe all of these scriptures are true. And so, at times when I've been hurting and unable to see Him at work anywhere in my life I have questioned "Why?"

One of those times occurred for me in February of 2014. Our family was in the car and a fight broke out. Sharp words cut back and forth exposing the raw edges of a reopened wound. There it was like a sealed off pocket of infection now oozing pus all over again. This was not a minor disagreement over what music to listen to or where to go for lunch. It was something I have cried and agonized over for years, praying hour upon hour. And in that moment, I saw no progress, no hope, no evidence of any answer to my prayers.

I have no doubt that Jesus could simply speak one word and this problem would cease to exist. That was exactly what made this hard. "Where was Jesus?"

Later that evening I was praying about this and I thought of Mary in John 11:1-44 where she asked Jesus to come and heal Lazarus. Jesus purposely chose not to come, and Lazarus died. Yes, He did come later, but Mary couldn't see the big picture yet and she felt totally abandoned by her Savior who could easily have healed him.

As I identified with Mary I prayed, "LORD, I feel just like Mary. Why didn't you come?" I then wondered, "What did He say to her in response?" I opened my Bible without knowing exactly where this story was and opened right to the exact verse where she expressed her feelings of abandonment. *"When Mary reached the place where Jesus was and saw him, she fell at his feet and said, "Lord, if you had been here, my brother would not have died."* (John 11:32) Realizing that God was truly wanting to answer me, my heart now stood at attention. What answer would He give me? *"When Jesus saw her weeping...he was deeply moved in his spirit and greatly troubled." John 11:33 ESV*

That was Jesus' response.

He didn't say to Mary, "You should have more faith." Or "Why are you mad at me?" No. He cared deeply about her heart. His heart broke for her because she trusted in Him and didn't understand His silence.

That word "troubled" in John 11:33 means "stirred up". His response to her emotions was to care passionately and want to swoop in and rescue her out of this pain. That to me is the goodness of God. He may have to move in ways I don't understand, but I can trust that He will never abandon me.

Good?

Lazarus died.
I run to hide.
Angry, bewildered,
My heart cries, "Why?
Why weren't You here LORD?
Why do You stay
Off in the distance
While I come and lay
My hope and my trust at Your feet.
You could have healed him
With just one word.
Your power is greater than I've even heard.
You healed the deaf man
And opened blind eyes.
You cast out demons
And silence the lies
Of any who challenge
Your mercy and grace
And desire to set free
All those bound in this place.
So why, Jesus, why?
I don't understand.
I know you are able...
Just one touch of Your hand...
Why didn't you come?"

*"When Jesus saw her weeping, and the Jews who had come along with
her also weeping, he was deeply moved in his spirit and greatly
troubled. And he said, "Where have you laid him?"*
John 11:33,34 ESV

"I want you to know, my dearest child,
That I have never left your side.
I'm walking with you through this pain.
My spirit burns and yearns to gain
That first deep breath of resurrection
Bursting forth complete redemption
I will breathe life into your dead.
My love for you has surely led
This painful four-day silence...

You do not know what I have planned.
The dead will rise at My command.
I will come in power for you
And you will see My glory too.

Like Moses who gazed upon My goodness,
Your eyes too will see the fullness
Of richest extravagant love lavished freely
Like perfume poured out
Waterfalls of pure mercy.
Even death is not the final word
Compassion rules; each cry I've heard.
I Am the Rock surrounding you,
The cleft where you are safe.
Wait here for My glory
For you will see my face."

*"Then Jesus, deeply moved again, came to the tomb. It was a cave,
and a stone lay against it. Jesus said, "Take away the stone.
John 11:38,39a ESV*

A Step Deeper In...

Have you been holding your heart back from the LORD because you've felt abandoned? Mary's story in John 11:1-44 invites us to bring those feelings of abandonment straight to the LORD. When Jesus came to Lazarus' town He specifically asked for Mary. He cared about her. Dare to come to Him and pour out your painful questions.

Chapter 14

FOUGHT FOR

WHEN I AM IN THE MIDDLE of an intense spiritual battle, I can feel a sense of free-falling, desperately grasping for something to hold onto. I feel helpless. A silent scream rises up in my inmost being crying out to be freed from the bombardment of Satan's lies and accusations. Fear and confusion close in and all I can do is cry out "Jesus, save me!"

When we find ourselves in such an experience, fear, shame, self-hatred, anger, depression - they seem to all gang up on us at once and they could take us down pretty quickly. At those times, where can we look to find security?

Song of Songs 2:4 AMP says, *"...his banner over me is love..."* Ancient armies would march in battalions under a specific flag and color that described and defined who they were, no matter how they performed. God has raised a flag, a banner, over us, and that banner is "love." That particular word used for love in this verse seems to mean "being in love."

What God is saying here is that He has raised a banner over each of us that says, "I am in love with this woman! And she is in love with me!" This truth is what we are to fix our eyes on when we are in a battle.

One of the names for God in scripture is Yahweh Nissi: The LORD My Banner. When I am in a battle and I look up at Jesus, I fix my eyes on who He is and who He has declared I am, His beloved. He is my Lover, my Mighty Warrior, the one who bought me with His blood, declaring victory for me in every battle I face.

In Bible times a banner was raised, not only to lead an army and declare their identity, but also to proclaim a victory already won. When I fix my eyes on Jesus, putting my faith completely in Him to save me, it's like that Banner snaps up into the sky and I am no longer in a freefall. I am held secure. Jesus has fought for me, and irrevocably won.

"You have shown your people desperate times; you have given us wine that makes us stagger. But for those who fear you, you have raised a banner to be unfurled against the bow." Psalm 60:3,4

THE UNSEEN

"So, we fix our eyes not on what is seen, but on what is unseen."
2 Corinthians 4:18a

There is a realm of reality that I cannot yet grasp
Where God is fighting for my soul, destroying Satan's clasp.
Those grimy nails no longer hold my life within their clutch.
His hold is in a hiss of lies that block me from God's touch.

"Where are You, God?" becomes my prayer,
but I hear no response.
"Please LORD, let me see Your face,
even just this once."

I stagger through a crowded room, my wobbly knees gone weak.
Chaos swirls about my head, Your Book pressed to my cheek.
Voices mock from everywhere, drowning out Your whisper.
I strain to feel Your beat of love pulsing through this leather.
Thirsty eyes reach out to me, "Will you give me a drink?"
My mind just spins out of control. I cannot see or think.

The battle is too much for me, I cry out "Jesus save me!"
Though my senses now are numb to God, I cannot stop believing.
A Banner is unfurled, snaps high into the sky.
God has given me a faith that I cannot deny.
Jesus is my Banner, and though the battle rages,
I fix my eyes upon His love, this God of all the ages.
"Though I can't seem to see You now,
nor hear You call my name...
I fix my eyes on The Unseen, my Warrior, untamed."

A Step Deeper In...

There is another verse that speaks of God fighting for us. *"...those who hope in me will not be disappointed. Can plunder be taken from warriors or captives rescued from the fierce? But this is what the LORD says: 'Yes, captives will be taken from warriors, and plunder retrieved from the fierce; I will contend with those who contend with you, and your children I will save.'" Isaiah 49:23b-25*

I love this promise that when we fix our eyes on Jesus, putting all our hope in Him, we will not be disappointed. He promises to fight for us, to return to us those things that have been stolen from us.

As my children have grown older, they have struggled with life's problems and much has been stolen from me and from them. If this is true of you also, I invite you to pray with me, "Jesus, my hope is in You! You are strong and mighty! Come and save my children!"

Chapter 15

SAFE

Jesus explained to His followers what it would take to draw close to Him. He said, *"Let the children come to me and do not hinder them, for to such belongs the kingdom of God. Truly, I say to you, whoever does not receive the kingdom of God like a child shall not enter it." Luke 18:16-17 ESV*

Little children are trusting. They eagerly receive the love offered to them without trying to earn it first. Other than being cute, they have nothing with which to pay for the things offered them. They simply come.

We are born trusting and so that must have been what I was like as a child, though I cannot remember. Somewhere along the way I learned to hide. I came to believe that I had to be good enough before I could receive love. I still struggle to sustain eye contact when revealing to another person the deep things of my heart. But I am less fearful than I used to be, not because I trust people more — but because I trust God more.

Jesus is a Secure Place of Safety that I have entered into. *"You are a hiding place for me; you preserve me from trouble; you surround me with shouts of deliverance." Psalm 32:7 ESV*

I am learning that when I am afraid I don't have to drop my gaze and hide inside myself. I can run into the safety of my Savior who knows me completely; every sin and failure, everything I've done wrong, every parenting mistake that affected my children. He stands tall behind me, smiling, and wraps His big strong arms around me. And He speaks out loud into my ear, in front of everyone, that I am forgiven and that He delights in me. *"All beautiful you are my darling; there is no flaw in you." (Song of Songs 4:7)* Outrageous grace!

Have you ever had a small child run to you for safety? His little muddy feet run right through the house without stopping to wipe at the door. He screams out your name with his outside voice, leaps into your arms and clings tightly to your neck with all his might, smearing his tears all over you. Something about such pure trust awakens a passion to protect that child no matter what.

When my son Simeon was little, he gave me a glimpse of what God must feel for us when we put our trust in Him. Simeon trusted me with his heart. There was nothing he could ever give me that would be more valuable to me. He could become President of the United States or discover a cure for cancer. He could be an Olympic gold medalist or a successful businessman, earning exorbitant amounts of money to give to the poor. None of that would ever surpass the value to me of the gift of his heart.

Because

*"...no wound was found on him
because he had trusted in his God."*
Daniel 6:23

Four-year-old trusting eyes
Run to me with no disguise.
"I'm safe with you," those eyes they say
How can I his trust betray?

Just last year he took a fall
While running carefree in the hall.
Childish, broke a well-known rule
And split his chin upon a stool.
His eyes reached up into my face
Knowing that he'd find there grace.
And as the needle formed each stitch
His eyes held mine with trust so rich.

I won't forget another day when he had just turned four;
Chocolate cake and presents, and friends around the floor.
The song began and in delight his eyes they searched for mine.
He trusted me to share his joy, our eyes and hearts entwined.
The song went on and line by line he never turned away.
Perfect trust, a priceless gift he gave to me that day.

Everything within me longs to meet his every need.
His trust awakens all my strength and for his life I'd bleed.
I pray that as the years go on through sad or joyful days,
Those trusting eyes will shift to God who never will betray.

A Step Deeper In...

Because our trust is precious to God, I believe He is eager to help us grow to trust Him more. Take time to pray that He will help you in this.

Chapter 16

HELD

As valuable to God as my trust is, the reality is that I cannot give Him perfect trust in my own strength. I am prone to wander, prone to distraction and fear, prone to the pride of thinking I can handle life on my own. I am totally dependent on the mercy and power of Jesus to free me, to lift my eyes toward Him.

The good news of the gospel is that one day we will be completely free of all these hindrances and we will be given perfect trust to offer Him. There will be nothing between us: no guilt, no shame, no fear, no unbelief, no pride, no veil. And the mystery is that how we will be, is also true of us now simply because we have asked the LORD God to forgive our sins and make us His child.

One day I was in the prayer room at the International House of Prayer in Kansas City. I was struggling to enter into worship and to come to some sense of His Presence. As my thoughts and emotions swirled around within me, striving to find peace and connection with God's love, God spoke clearly to me. It was a quick, subtle picture in my mind, breaking through the desperation and bringing peace and joy and freedom.

I believe it was Jesus. He knelt before me and looked deep into my eyes with such tenderness and joy and He said, "You can't do it wrong, Honey!" Here I was striving to trust Him more, to focus on Him intensely, to somehow make myself more pleasing to Him that I would find intimacy with Him. In that one moment, I knew that I could do nothing to gain more access to Him.

And I could do nothing to prevent it. He was saying "You're clean! You're Mine! You can come to me however you want to! You are totally completely righteous, independent of what you do. However you try to come to me, you're in!"

Even now as I try to explain this I know I'm not even touching the reality of grace. It is way more than we can know now. There is a union with God that came when we were born into His family. We received His DNA. We are walking forever intertwined with Him. As you walk with Him, my prayer is that He will keep you looking into His eyes, trusting His love, fascinated with His glory.

We could walk with someone through life and yet never really connect at the heart level if we're always looking away from that person to other pursuits. It's gazing into the eyes that brings intimacy. And what a waste it would be to walk through life intertwined with Christ, but missing intimacy.

Leaning Eyes

"Who is this coming up from the wilderness
leaning on her beloved?"
Song of Songs 8:5

Hand in hand, LORD, arm in arm —
This union saves me from all harm.
Every cell intertwined,
For I am Yours and You are mine.
As I walk with You this way
Hold my chin, Dear LORD, I pray
For I am prone to look away
And drop my gaze, LORD make me stay
Focused, steady, eyes-in-eyes
Undistracted, undisguised.

A Step Deeper In...

What does "intimacy with Jesus" look like anyway? I know I touch upon it in my life, but not with the consistency and depth I long for. When I take an honest look at my walk with the LORD, I feel like I've barely begun to know Him.

Intimacy is when we are unveiled to someone; raw, all pretense stripped away, seen for who we are, and loved. It's that rare place of knowing that we are truly loved just as we are. It requires risk, vulnerability and humility; all things we don't step into easily.

The only way into intimacy with Jesus is when He first unveils Himself to us; when He gives us just a tiny glimpse of His beauty. He might do that through a song or a scripture, an answered prayer, or the words of a friend.

When I realize I've lost the sense of intimacy with Jesus, the way back is to ask Him again for another glimpse of His beauty—and then I watch and saturate myself with scripture until I see Him afresh again. That glimpse ignites in me humility and trust.

How about you? How do you experience intimacy with Jesus? Spend some time in prayer, asking Jesus to help you see Him anew. Then watch for Him. Watching for Jesus can take many forms, some of which include reading His Word, hearing it preached, fasting and prayer, stepping out to follow Him in obedience, worship, resting, solitude, or spending time with other believers or alone with God in nature. Remember how you last saw Him. Maybe that is the place to begin watching again.

Chapter 17

SECURE

ONE DAY MY SON told me I was a control freak. I was initially offended. I don't agree with all his thinking regarding that accusation, but as much as I hate to admit it - I am. I know that the need for control can take many forms. But, underlying most or even all of those forms is not so much a need to control, but rather the need for a sense of security.

When I feel out of control my house gets cleaned. I deep clean closets and drawers, ruthlessly throwing things out and giving things away. At least then there is one area of my life in order, a place to hold onto when the rest of me is floundering.

On a deeper level, when people or things that have given me a sense of security are taken from me, I feel anxiety, even a near panic sometimes. What can I hold onto now? Will God really take care of me? The bottom line is "CAN I TRUST YOU GOD?"

It amazes me that even after walking with God now for nearly 50 years, and seeing His faithfulness over and over, when everything topples, that question still pokes out of the rubble and I find myself staring straight into it again. I find I need an anchor, something to hold my soul at those times.

"We have this hope as an anchor for the soul, firm and secure." *(Hebrews 6:19a)* Hebrews is believed to have been written prior to the fall of Jerusalem in A.D. 70. It would prepare the early believers for the destruction of the temple and all their religious systems, and the sacrifices and priests.

No longer would they have these things to lean on for their spiritual security. There would be no person to intercede for them before God, no priest. They needed to know beyond any doubt that Jesus was their priest now. They could go directly to God's throne in prayer at any time, because Jesus was the final sacrifice for their sins. They needed to know that Jesus was all that was required, no matter what else was taken away.

I decided to write out exactly what my hope is, to have it firmly fixed in my mind and heart so that I can easily grab onto it whenever I begin to flounder in my faith. As I proceeded to do this, forming it into a poem, it came alive to me. This poem is for me a fiery statement of faith, a creed that I can recite when my faith begins to waver.

The lies may come and with them the doubts. When everything topples I may have to take a while to stare again into that big, scary question, but because of the Gospel of Jesus Christ I have something that the world does not have. I have an anchor. These recited truths are my anchor, thrust hard and deep into the ocean floor, securing my soul in God's love.

THE HOPE I PROFESS

*"Let us hold unswervingly to the hope we profess,
for he who promised is faithful."*
Hebrews 10:23

I have a Savior restoring my soul
And He will not stop until I am whole.
I have a Warrior fighting for me
Loosing sin's hold and setting me free.
I have a Bridegroom
In love with me now
Though my mind cannot
Understand why or how.

Ravished, pursuing me,
Wanting to speak with me,
Whispering mysteries,
Drawing me near.

I am not of this world
I was made for Another...
Made for a Lover. There is no other
Who'll enter my soul and satisfy
The lonely depths of my heart's cry.

For flesh of His flesh, formed from His side
I was made only in Him to abide.
I was made for a Man riding on a white horse
"Like a champion rejoicing to run His course."
As my eyes meet His gaze for the first time that day
What I will behold words could simply not say.

In the blaze of His passion, my heart will be free
To worship my Lover with all that's in me.

I long for You, Jesus. Come quickly, my King.
I ache to give You everything.

Psalm 23:3, Exodus 15:1-18, Song of Songs 4:9-10; 7:10,
Genesis 2:22-24, Revelation 19:11-16, Psalm 19:5

A Step Deeper In...

Have you ever taken the time to write out exactly what the hope is that you profess? If this poem adequately expresses your hope, you are certainly free to memorize it and use it as I do. But maybe you'd like to write out your own anchor. It doesn't have to be a poem, but it will be most useful if it's something you can memorize so it's there whenever you need it.

Chapter 18

RESTORED

"HE RESTORES MY SOUL." (*Psalm 23:3 ESV*) I don't know exactly what this means in relation to God as our shepherd, but when I think of God restoring my soul I picture Him as a craftsman restoring an old piece of furniture. In my limited study of furniture restoration I have learned that the primary requirement is patience.

Many who want to undertake restoring something are put off by the amount of work involved. Such projects cannot be completed in one day. In scripture, wood is symbolic for humanity, so there must be parallels here between restoring wood and restoring our souls.

The first step of restoration usually entails cleaning the piece thoroughly with an oil that washes away all the dust and grime it's collected throughout its life. The job is tedious, but the craftsman undertakes such a work because he enjoys it. He is creative by nature. He is patient. Ideally, he knows the story behind each piece of furniture he restores. He knows how each crack was formed and where all that dirt came from. He knows exactly when that knob broke off and when someone tried to cover up its scratches with that thick coat of paint. He is patient because he knows that he is restoring a masterpiece!

God looks at us as a craftsman would eye a piece of furniture needing to be restored. He sees beneath the grime and knows the beauty that lies hidden underneath. In tender love, He gently pours over our hearts the oil of the Holy Spirit and washes us clean in the blood of Jesus. Then He patiently works to repair the brokenness, replace the missing parts, and bring out the long-hidden beauty of our souls. For us the process is long; it takes a lifetime.

He Restores My Soul

Psalm 23:3

I have a Savior restoring my soul
Unceasing mercy remaking me whole.
A Craftsman working by candlelight,
Relentlessly pressing through the night.

Anticipating, consumed with zeal,
A masterpiece dawn will reveal.
Pouring the Oil, rubbing it in,
Stripping old paint worn so thin
Revealing a beauty there at the start
When I was born in His heart.
Years of brokenness washed away
By the blood of the One
Who bought me that day.

Precious Lord, my whole soul sings
Praise to You, my Savior King.

A Step Deeper In...

Let the first sentence of this poem wash over you; think about it for a while. It is liberating.

Chapter 19

PURSUED

THERE HAVE BEEN SEASONS in my walk with God where I have been totally consumed with love for Him. There is nothing more exhilarating to me than feeling God's love and being in love with Him.

But there have also been seasons in my walk with God where that passion has disappeared. The awareness of His Presence and the sound of His voice became hard to access. The sense of being totally consumed with love for Him slowly faded.

Gradually I found myself more and more drawn to food for comfort, feeling unfulfilled with my life, wanting to go shopping, or dissatisfied with my marriage because it was not meeting my needs. Why?

The answer is not always the same. But at times the answer can be found in the book of Hosea where God calls the prophet Hosea to not only speak of God's love for His people, but to actually live out a picture of it for us. God called Hosea to marry a woman who would be unfaithful to him. Through Hosea's lifelong faithfulness to pursuing her, God was showing His people His relentless loving commitment to them. God has chosen an adulterous bride. That's us. We are easily distracted from the LORD by all the worldly pleasures that confront us.

Sometimes we consciously choose to turn away from God to someone or something in our lives that we think we can trust more to satisfy our souls in the moment. Other times it is a very subtle process of being lured away to the many good things that can consume our time and energy and leave our intimacy with the LORD waiting in the background.

When this happens to me, at some point I wake up and realize I'm in someone else's bed, and my soul is no longer satisfied. What do I do then? Guilt rushes in to try to keep me from crying out to the true Lover of my soul. I wonder how He could ever want me back.

But God wrote the book of Hosea for those moments. The fact that I even want to return to God shows He is already wooing me back. *"Therefore, I am now going to allure her; I will lead her into the wilderness and speak tenderly to her." Hosea 2:14*

"Go, show your love to your wife again, though she is loved by another man and is an adulteress. Love her as the LORD loves the Israelites, though they turn to other gods and love the sacred raisin cakes." Hosea 3:1

God chose the prophet Hosea to marry a prostitute and thus proclaim to the world His passionate love for sinful humans who forget Him and chase after other loves to try to satisfy their souls. He pursues them and woos them until they are completely His. His promise to us is that He will heal our waywardness and we will one day enjoy the unending exhilaration of the romance we were created for; the mystery of the Gospel of Jesus Christ!

Hosea*

"Like a lily among thorns is my darling among the young women."
Song of Songs 2:2

"...with Your blood You purchased people for God..."
Revelation 5:9 AMP

Naked, she stood there empty-eyed
Numb to the pain shrouded inside
The skin-deep beauty that covered her soul
A bouquet of dried flowers set over a hole
Where a baby was buried before she became
The beautiful Lily dreamed in her name.

A life of adultery, given for free
Long-denied longings for someone to see
Under the make-up veiling her face
And respond with a true unfailing embrace.

Now she was being sold once again
Led bound to the block and judged by men
Who tried to estimate her worth
Though blinded by the lusts of earth.
They could not see what Jesus saw—
His Lily buried 'neath the straw
And dirt and filth that covered her
The passion of His heart was stirred.
"I want this woman! She is Mine!
She is the bride of My design."
With zeal, He stepped out through the crowd,
His eyes locked into hers.

The emptiness that marked her face
began to fill with tears.
His gaze, a warmth her frozen heart
had never known before.
The dormant bloom inside her stirred,
"Could there really be a Door?
Someone to open up this tomb and lead me out to play
And dance and sing and feel again
the colors of the day?"
Boldly, Jesus took her hand and for her life He paid...

a holy price.

He knelt right there and at her feet He laid
Every drop of His own blood poured out for all to see.
He purchased her and whispered
"Come away, and marry Me."

*"I will heal their waywardness and love them freely,
for my anger has turned away from them.
I will be like the dew to Israel; he will blossom like a lily."*
Hosea 14:4,5a

* Hosea means "Salvation"

A Step Deeper In...

Read the book of Hosea asking God to speak to you about His passionate love for you.

Chapter 20

ROMANCED

ONE THING

*"One thing I ask from the LORD, this only do I seek: that I may dwell
in the house of the LORD all the days of my life, to gaze on the beauty
of the LORD and to seek him in his temple."*
Psalm 27:4

There is a Romance, a Holy Dance,
Hidden beneath the noise...of daily routine.
Pray, eat, shower, laundry,
Dishes, feed cat, clean spilled jelly.
Dust, eat, schoolwork, vacuum,
Mend a jacket, scrub the bathroom.
Pay the bills, balance the books,
Sweep the floors, don't miss the nooks.

Check email, return phone calls,
Scan sales flyers from the malls.
Break up fights, turn off lights,
Boil potatoes, freeze tomatoes.
Pray, eat, try to teach
The things that really matter.
All the while, underneath,
Somewhere deep down and beneath
The ordinariness of life
Woven throughout all that clatter
Lies One Thing that really matters.
There is a Romance, a Holy Dance
A following the lead.
A leaning close to hear Him whisper
Or just to feel Him breathe
His Spirit into mindless tasks.
He moves in the mundane,
As well as in the crisis
And the times of deepest pain.

Open my eyes LORD, that I may see
You in the middle of daily routine.

ROMANCE IS WHAT MAKES us come alive. It is what we were made for; to love and be loved, to be totally consumed with delight in Another Who is totally consumed with delight in us. It is an adventure of being wooed, lavishly pursued, simply enjoyed. Romance is a string of gifts and surprises and tender affection, enjoyed by a couple in secret, even though they may be surrounded by people. Romance can be witnessed, but it can truly only be fully experienced by those who are romancing or being romanced.

I remember the first time someone said to me, "I have a word from God for you." She proceeded to share with me a scripture that pierced my heart. This amazing thought that the God of all creation had noticed me and had spoken directly to me, personally—this blew me away. How could He love me this much, to speak to me, a nobody?

This gift from Jesus ushered me into a hunger for more and more of Him. I began seeking Him through reading the Bible, listening to other believers, Christian radio, worship songs and prayer. I asked Him to tell me what He's like through the things He created in nature.

And the more I hungered for Him and sought to hear His voice, the more I found Him giving me little glimpses of His Presence and His love for me. He was romancing me.

I have found that I cannot go very long without romance in my relationship with Christ. I quickly lose passion for Him if I lose touch with this romance of the gospel. When that happens, I must seek Him.

I pull away from the noise of life to get alone with Him and I listen for His voice. I set my heart to obey whatever He tells me. I cry out to Him to draw me away with Him again. I pray through

the Song of Songs. I watch for Him. And He surprises me again...
in secret...and my heart revives.

As I meditated on Song of Songs 2:8-10 I was impressed with
the closeness of Jesus as I go through my daily routine.

> *"Listen! My beloved!*
> *Look! Here he comes,*
> *leaping across the mountains, bounding over the hills.*
> *My beloved is like a gazelle or a young stag.*
> *Look! There he stands behind our wall,*
> *gazing through the windows, peering through the lattice.*
> *My beloved spoke and said to me,*
> *"Arise, my darling, my beautiful one,*
> *come with me."*
> *Song of Songs 2:8-10*

I am a homemaker and spend my days mostly within the house.
As I move from room to room I imagine Him right there with me.
I imagine Him right on the other side of the wall, right outside my
window, watching me and my family intimately, ready to act on
our behalf.

Our imaginations are a gift from God to help us access spiritual things. As long as we are grounded in scripture and do not
allow our imaginations to go against scriptural truth, I believe God
speaks to us through this vehicle.

This is how I write and how an artist paints. This is how we enter
into the romance of the gospel. It involves much more of us than
mere intellectual assent to truth. It is a falling in love. Whoever
did that without their imagination? I have heard it said something
like, "Oh, that's just emotionalism." But it's impossible to fall in
love without abundant emotions.

In Christian circles, there are many voices telling us of all the things we need to be doing to serve Jesus. And everywhere we look there are needs to be met; people who need love or food or shelter or teaching or help of some kind.

Is it okay to take time for romance in our relationship with Jesus? Anyone who's been married awhile knows that romance doesn't just happen. It has to be cultivated, a place made for it. It requires relaxed time alone with a person. And without it, passion fades.

When Jesus was asked what was the most important commandment, He replied *"Love the Lord your God with all your heart and with all your soul and with all your mind." (Matthew 22:36,37)* He is telling us that what God wants above all else is for us to love Him with all our affections, desires, feelings, passions, thoughts, imagination, and intellectual capacity. Actively falling more in love with Jesus, cultivating romance with Him, should be our top priority.

One day I was praying that God would let me hear His heartbeat (symbolically, that I would connect with what He is most passionate about.) I sensed Him say to me, "If you want to hear my heartbeat, you have to lay upon my chest and let me hold you." In essence He was saying, "You can't hear My heartbeat from a distance."

Before you read this poem, I invite you to prayerfully study Song of Songs 2:3-10. The more understanding we have of the symbols in Song of Songs, the more confidence and delight we can have in the truths of these verses. Studying and praying through Song of Songs has been the most powerful way for me to access the experiential awareness of Jesus' love.

THE SERENADE

"As an apple tree among the trees of the forest so is my beloved among the young men. With great delight I sat in his shadow, and his fruit was sweet to my taste. He brought me to the banqueting house, and his banner over me was love." Song of Songs 2:3,4 ESV

Long before dawn, she lights a lamp
And sits alone in the stillness.
A busy day waits, but before the dawn breaks,
She lingers here under the apple tree.
The room isn't much—a table, a chair,
A window o'erlooking the city.
But here she is served royal hors d'oeuvres,
Just a foretaste of her wedding banquet.
Her Bible propped open upon her lap,
Across her shoulders a banner
To cover her shame and declare that she
Belongs to the Love Who bought her...
Who fought for her freedom and woos her now
With this love song He sings through the lattice.

Here I stand watching you,
From a realm beyond your grasp...
Just beyond the lattice
That I've made to hold Me back.
For I would come upon you now;
My love has been aroused.
You cannot bear My glory yet
And so I have you housed
Within the lattice shielding you
From light too bright to bear

Desire flashing from My eyes
And flowing through My hair.
Your mortal flesh could not contain
The fire upon My face.
It's kindled deep and overflows
Like sunrays piercing space.
For in My heart I hold for you
A love like none you've known—
And for its pleasures you were made.
You will be My Own.

Whatever obstacles arise
To standing close beside My bride—
I leap and bound over them all,
Laughing, for they are too small
To try to block you from My love.
I blow a kiss, a flutter, My Dove
Slides through the veil to give to you
Comfort, joy and power too.

This lattice mesh restricts your sight
But always through the day or night
Though My glory is held back
I whisper through the lattice cracks
That I am yours and you are Mine
And one day soon there'll be a time
When I will run to you and say
"Arise, my darling, come away"
Come run with Me upon the heights
And dance with Me in broad daylight!
The lattice has been torn in two!
Come, the Dawn has broken through!

A Step Deeper In...

Jesus not only watches us, but He also invites us to come run with Him. He reaches out His hand to us in our safe places of security and comfort and invites us to go on adventures with Him that are beyond our ability to envision, places where we have to trust Him completely.

This is the sort of thing that the best romantic movies are made of; the lovely maiden bravely joins the strong, valiant warrior as they together gallop away on a handsome horse to defeat the enemy. The romance is all wrapped up in the adventure. In fact, it begins with the watching but culminates in the adventure.

When we find ourselves longing to be romanced again by Jesus, maybe He is already beckoning to us, "Arise, my darling, my beautiful one, and come with me." Is there a step out into the unknown that He is drawing you to take with Him?

Chapter 21

GIVEN TRUTH

ONE DAY JESUS WILL INDEED call us to arise and "Come dance with Me in broad daylight!" But for now, we dance with Him in the dark. We have to sense His leanings through the touch of the Holy Spirit and listen closely for His whispers, or we will not be able to follow.

As overwhelmingly exhilarating as that dance in broad daylight will be, I wonder if there are treasures of intimacy that can only be learned in long nights of dancing with Him in pitch darkness.

I must confess, I would not choose the dark. I long for broad daylight more than I can possibly put into words. But I also want the treasures that He has hidden for me in the secret places of the dark.

Just as a deaf person learns to feel the music and a blind person learns to hear the slightest sound, I believe the LORD is opening up our spiritual senses in a way that we might never be able to know Him if we grew up in full light.

I believe the testimonies of people who have heard God's audible voice or have seen vivid dreams or open visions of Jesus. As much as I long for those things, I have not yet experienced them. But for all eternity I will never again be able to give to Jesus what can only be given in the darkness—faith without sight. And so, when I cannot see Jesus, I am practicing turning my heart up to Him and offering Him my love and trust. I believe that He receives it as a precious gift.

"Your word is a lamp for my feet, a light on my path." (*Psalm 119:105*) As I walk in the darkness, the light of God's Word leads me. Sometimes the lies that bombard me each day block the light, like layer upon layer of black tape placed over the head of a flashlight. If I am alert and strong I can fight them off fairly easily. But if I'm tired, hungry, lonely, angry, sick or any number of other conditions that I often find myself in, it takes discipline and crying out to God for help, to offer Jesus that gift of faith without sight.

Now

"Arise, come, my darling; my beautiful one,
come with me...catch for us the foxes,
the little foxes that ruin the vineyards...
Until the day breaks and the shadows flee,
turn, my beloved, and be like a gazelle
or like a young stag on the rugged hills."
Song of Songs 2:13,15,17

Pitch black, I cannot see.
Lying foxes snarl at me.
Deceit's dark voices shroud my ear.
The Serenade I cannot hear.
I have a choice to make tonight.
God's Word is here in black and white.
Truth takes my hand and whispers "Come."
How can I when I feel so numb
To any sense of God right now?
"Arise...and come...I'll show you how.
We'll catch the foxes one by one.
Now is the time to arise and come.
It's not when day breaks and the shadows flee
It's now you must "turn" and run with Me."

A Step Deeper In...

Choose to believe the truth that God is calling you to believe. Ask Him for scripture verses to hold onto, verses that declare the truth. Ask Him to increase your faith and take one step that requires you to believe.

Chapter 22

FASCINATED

As WE PEEL AWAY the dark layers of the lies of the enemy, there remains the darkness of yearning and searching for the God of Whom we cannot sustain a clear vision until heaven.

Being without Christ is like being blindfolded alone in a windowless, soundproof, closed closet. I have found dancing with Christ to be like having my eyes closed while outside in the daytime. I can't see, but I can tell there's light. I can follow it. I can tell when something's blocking it, and when I turn my face directly to the sun, it's almost too bright.

This is the darkness of yearning and searching for God. We can sense the light, feel its warmth, but long to be able to open our eyes and see clearly all the wonders we know from scripture to be true of God. We may catch momentary glimpses of some of these wonders as if for an instant one of our eyelids cracked slightly open. But we dream of what it will be like to finally open our eyes.

We can spend this time on earth, the time of closed eyes, inside our houses just sitting and waiting in silence, or we can step out through the door of faith and believe that if we seek God He will reveal more of Himself to us. We still won't see as much as we long to see, but maybe we will feel the cool, wet grass tickling our bare feet, and hear the music of hundreds of birds and frogs and crickets singing. We may feel the wind toss through our hair and an occasional brave butterfly rest on our shoulders. As we link arms with others who, with closed eyelids have also stepped out of their houses into the adventure of exploring what they cannot quite see, together we stumble into a brightness we might never experience alone.

Nearly every time I open God's Word to seek Him, I pray Hebrews 11:6 *"...anyone who comes to him (God) must believe that he exists and that he rewards those who earnestly seek him."*

I pray, "God, I believe that You exist and that You reveal yourself to those who earnestly seek You." I also pray Psalm 119:18 *"Open my eyes that I may see wonderful things in your law."* The good news of the gospel is that I can know God *now.*

I don't have to wait for Heaven, living bored until I get there. I was created to live fascinated.

But God has chosen to fascinate me as I *seek* Him. He wants me to go after Him with all my heart. He wants to be discovered, uncovered and mined.

There Is a Mine...

Job 28

Digging through this holy darkness
Far beneath the light of day.
Stealing away from the ones I cherish,
All the loves that bid me stay
Above the ground and miss the treasures
Hidden deep beyond this earth—
Gold and silver, nuggets of Wisdom,
Glimpses of God of utmost worth.

Tunneling down into the silence
Alone, I fear the quietness.
But in the silence, Springs are waiting,
Streams that flood my loneliness.
Diamonds, all their sides of splendor,
Glints of God's glorious majesty.
"No eye has seen, no ear has heard"
His secrets waiting still for me.

Jesus, Your Living Word—my headlight,
Voice that splits in two the night,
Lead me into Your thoughts and passions
Views of Your glory awaiting my sight.
I'll dangle and sway on cords of mercy,
Held securely by each string.
I'll shout upon each newfound treasure
Virgin praise for You, my King.
I'll cut a shaft far from where people dwell.
Solitude, such a forgotten way.
A secret adventure to know my Lover—
This romance until our wedding day.

There is a Mine...and I will mine it.
LORD, take me deep into You, I pray.

A Step Deeper In...

Mining is a learned skill. One doesn't tunnel down into the depths of a cave without tools and a plan. I don't remember for sure who taught me this, but one of my best "mining techniques" has been the "read it, write it, say it, sing it, pray it" method.

I read the Word and watch for a verse to be highlighted to me, something I want to know more deeply or believe more surely. I write that verse out on an index card. I take it out with me on walks day after day and I talk to God about it phrase by phrase. Singing it sometimes helps slow down my thoughts and open up my emotions.

Through this process that verse becomes a part of me, going over and over within me as I go through my day and even through the night. I now can feel its power and see new things about God that I didn't see before or see old things afresh.

Yes, it takes work. If I waited until I felt like digging I wouldn't do it. In mining, there is a lot of time spent just searching. Some days one finds nothing, some a single treasure, but then some days the edges of a huge store of jewels are uncovered and it takes weeks to bring them all out.

Those days are more exciting to me than anything in the whole world, and so I keep searching for more, because... He's worth it.

Chapter 23

DELIGHTED IN

When God reveals Himself to the human spirit it is intoxicating. One taste and I am addicted. Every revelation of God is a revelation of love. *"...God is love." (1 John 4:8)* I cannot see Him without seeing His love for me.

I used to think of God's love in general terms, like "God loves the world, so He loves me because I'm part of the world." But the more revelation I receive of God, the more personal His affection for me becomes.

Humans like to show personal affection for someone by calling him or her a special name. People spend a lot of time deciding what to name a child. Everyone in the family weighs in with their suggestions. My middle son can be grateful we didn't listen to his older brother who wanted to name him Black-eyed Bart.

I remember oftentimes daydreaming about what to name the next baby, diving into different possibilities with name meanings and consequences. As the child grows into school-age and then into adulthood, would the name always fit?

God has chosen to name His children also. God says to every one of His children *"...you shall be called by a new name that the mouth of the LORD will give." Isaiah 62:2 ESV*

What process must God have gone through in deciding what to name His bride? Unlike us He could see the end from the beginning and He knew every day in between. With perfect knowledge of who we would be, He chose the perfect name.

God declares *"...you shall be called My Delight Is in Her...for the LORD delights in you... as the bridegroom rejoices over the bride so shall your God rejoice over you." Isaiah 62:4,5 ESV*

A bridegroom rejoicing over a bride...that is the picture God has given us of how much He delights in us.

I think my favorite part of a wedding is watching the groom's face as he takes in the sight of his bride as she begins to make her way down the aisle. One man delighting in one woman, his entire body brimming over with passionate emotions. He can't take his eyes off this girl who he has pursued, wooed and waited for. He is overwhelmed with intense desire to take her to himself, totally ravished with her beauty.

That, Beloved, is a tiny earthly glimpse of how Jesus feels about you, from the moment you say "yes" to Him.

The Hebrew word for "My Delight Is in Her" is "Hephzibah." If this is God's name for His bride, then this is His name for each of us. When we pray, "Jesus?" He answers, "Yes, Hephzibah?" He wants us to know personally that His delight in us has given us a new name.

If you are trusting in Jesus as your Savior, then you are His bride and He calls you "Hephzibah" too.

Listen! Your Bridegroom is calling your name.

Listen! Mercy's Pounding on My Door!

"I slept but my heart was awake. Listen!
My beloved is knocking:
"Open to me, my sister, my darling, my dove, my flawless one."
Song of Songs 5:2

Blinded by darkness I cannot see.
My ears can't hear you speak to me.
Numb to You, my body sleeps,
But deep within my spirit leaps
Like John the Baptist in the womb!
You've come! You've risen from the tomb!
Your heartbeat pounds upon my door.
I burn and yearn for You, my Lord.

You are alive! I know You're here.
I can't explain how I feel You near.
But You're knocking and pounding and calling my name...
Joyful, delighting, a child in the rain...
Tongue catching raindrops, wide open grin,
Wet, barefoot toes a wigglin'!
Bouncing knees and feet leaping high,
Nail-scarred hands extend to the sky!
Jumping and splashing and laughing out loud,
Waiting for me beneath a cloud.
A rainbow of mercy stored up to pour down.
If I will just stop
To hear the sound—

"Listen! My lover is knocking..."

He wants me! Oh, how He wants you too!
There is no frown on His face towards you.
He paid the price for all your sin.
It's gone! Now there's nothing between you and Him,
Only this door of your heart.
And He says to you now, with that grin of delight...
"You can't do it wrong, Honey...I've made you right."

"You...delight to show mercy."
Micah 7:18

"For the LORD takes delight in his people..."
Psalm 149:4

A Step Deeper In...

Memorize Psalm 149:4.

Chapter 24

COMMISSIONED

WHEN I EXPERIENCE SOME TOUCH of God's love, it can feel too good to be true, like I must be dreaming. I live for those days. But then there are the dry times, where I hold onto God by replaying the memories. Psalm 126 begins with the people of God remembering one of those dreamlike days and asking God to do it again. *"When the LORD restored the fortunes of Zion, we were like those who dream. Then our mouth was filled with laughter and our tongue with shouts of joy." Psalm 126:1,2 ESV*

The Psalm closes with a promise. It says that when we sow the seed God gives us, we will reap a harvest with great joy. It seems that God is showing us a link between sowing seed and reaping the joy of fresh revelation of His goodness.

Beth Moore teaches on this Psalm in her book *Stepping Up.* (LifeWay Press, 2007, p.81) She speaks of a time when she visited a poverty-stricken country with widespread starvation. The great frustration of a missionary leader in that country was that when the people were given seed they would eat it rather than plant it and bring forth the harvest.

I have been one who is guilty of eating the seed. I just want to hear God and know Him, one discovery after another, but I can be slow to step out and take the risks and do the work required to sow what He gives me. As I pray for Jesus to once again "fill my mouth with laughter and my tongue with shouts of joy," maybe God's answer comes in a sack of seed.

Jesus told a parable about sowing seed. In it He identified the seed as the word of God. He explained that when God's word is sown in people's hearts, *"those with a noble and good heart...hear the word, retain it, and by persevering produce a crop." (Luke 8:15)* God wants us to *do* something with His words.

I want to esteem God's words so highly that I refuse to let any of them be lost. Whether it's a word of scripture, a gentle nudging of the Holy Spirit upon my conscience, or a word He speaks to me in prayer, God's words are valuable seeds. If I cultivate them, over time they will produce a crop.

Jesus also invites us to join Him in sowing these valuable seeds into other people's hearts. In fact, He has commissioned us to do so. *"Go into all the world and preach the gospel to all creation." (Mark 16:15)* "Gospel" is a word that carries the meaning "good news." Sowing seed, sharing God's good news is not merely our job; it's our link to joy. *"Those who sow in tears shall reap with shouts of joy!" Psalm 126:5 ESV*

Sometimes we sow our seeds in tears. Do you know what that's like? It's the perseverance it takes to sow when it's just plain back-breaking work, with hard soil and no hint of a harvest in sight. For me it meant loving a child like I'd never loved anyone before, teaching him God's words day after day, yet having him pull against me, rebel in anger, veer off the path and crash. As I painfully watch the unfolding of devastating consequences in his life, sowing in tears means that I stay soft. It means continuing to love though my heart is breaking. It means I dig down deep into God's Word to find fresh faith each day, as I continue praying for him and entrusting him to God.

Whatever "sowing in tears" means in each of our lives, such perseverance comes with a promise... we "shall reap with shouts of joy!" Where I have sown in tears, I am anticipating a mammoth heaping truckload-full of joy. Because God keeps His word.

"Let us not become weary in doing good, for at the proper time we will reap a harvest if we do not give up." Galatians 6:9

ONE SACK

"...the seed is the word of God."
Luke 8:11b

One sack of seed per hungry man...
What will you do with this gift of My hand?
Will you fill your belly, lie down and sleep
Or sow in the dirt, a harvest to reap?
Each seed tastes sweet, we can admire
Or fall to our knees in our mud and mire
And plant that word deep in total surrender
Choosing to follow Jesus, The Sower.

Across the room a young man hides
His eyes and his heart beneath the guise
Of apathy and disrespect,
A scream for help to resurrect
The life he's lost and can't retrieve...
A field of dirt, ripe for seed.
Down the street, a newborn cries.
A mother tries to silence the lies
That tell her she really has no hope
Of raising a child when she cannot cope
With a dying marriage and so many needs...
A field of dirt, ripe for seed.
One tiny seed, a simple word, a single act of
kindness heard
Slips beneath the filthy soil,
A silent, unseen flask of oil.
Holy Spirit power unleashed

Begins to grow to full release.
Time will show each word that's sown
Will multiply a hundred-fold.

Some seeds are whispers, "Give her a hug."
"Walk over to him and ask him to lunch."
If we turn away, that seed dies in the sack.
We may not ever get the chance back.
God's Word stills hunger for a day
Or forever when we choose to pay
The price of sowing each seed deep,
Persevering in faith, a harvest to reap.

Each truth applied, though in tears,
Cultivated through days or years
In the dirt of our lives or those that we know...

When God gives us seed it's meant
to be sown.

"...hear the word, retain it, and by
persevering, produce a crop."
Luke 8:15b

A Step Deeper In...

Can you identify "a field of dirt ripe for seed" anywhere near you? Go ahead... sow a seed.

Chapter 25

LED

Sowing seed effectively requires being led by the Holy Spirit. In order for a seed to take root, grow and eventually produce fruit, the season, timing and soil conditions, among other things, need to be right. So, what does it look like to be led by the Holy Spirit?

"But thanks be to God, who in Christ always leads us in triumphal procession, and through us spreads the fragrance of the knowledge of him everywhere." 2 Corinthians 2:14 ESV

The good news of the gospel is that God will always lead us. Most noticeably, He does this through scripture. For example, if a homeless, starving child comes to our door, God has already led us through scripture to feed the child and care for his needs.

But then what? From here we must listen to the inward voice of the Holy Spirit as we seek to discern how God is leading us to minister to this child. Someone once described this inward voice as "a little thought right next to my own." The more we know the scriptures, the easier it is to recognize the origin of those thoughts because God's voice will always line up with scripture.

Still, learning to discern the voice of the Holy Spirit is a learning process, more often cloudy than clear. And it also involves a growing trust that God will lead us on the best path even when our sense of His leading is cloudy. My experience has been that my trust grows most through looking behind me after I've taken steps through the fog trying to follow His lead. The path behind is often clearer.

Some people love to lead. I like to follow. Give me someone trustworthy to follow and I feel secure. I have always searched for mentors. My childhood mentor who, as I grew up, became my dear friend, died a few years back. There is a void in my life that remains to this day. I miss her.

That is the problem with mentors. They will not always be there. And they, being human, will not always lead me perfectly. Thus, they can help, but they cannot bring the security I crave.

But there is One who can. Jesus says to me, "Come, follow me." Many people look at Christianity as a list of rules. They feel they would be fenced in by it, rather than set free. But Jesus says, *"I am the way..." John 14:6*

The way to life is a Person, a Relationship, a Lover. And He promises to never leave us or forsake us no matter how lost we may feel at times. Jesus will lead us *always* whether we can see Him ahead of us or not. We can trust that His leading does not depend on our ability to see Him, only on our choice to follow even where we cannot see.

When Jesus leads me to step out of my comfort zone to plant a seed in someone's life, I do not go merely in my own strength. The Holy Spirit actually lives inside me.

"But you will receive power when the Holy Spirit comes on you; and you will be my witnesses..." (Acts 1:8) The awareness of that power turns my weak and timid personality into one eager to rush into the darkness with God's bright, life-giving Presence.

Hidden within a familiar Bible story, Jesus has painted a picture for us of what it is to carry His Presence to the lost. This picture becomes visible by imagining what it must have been like to be the donkey Jesus chose to ride on as He entered Jerusalem to save his people from their sins.

The young donkey Jesus chose had never been ridden before, thus he must have been naturally skittish and difficult to lead. But when Jesus touched him—a touch that radiated love and healing power, unlike anything he had ever known, the donkey knew he was safe.

Jesus' bringing salvation to lost souls was never about the donkey's talents or charismatic personality. It was all about the powerful Presence the humble donkey carried.

CARRYING HIS PRESENCE

"Fear not, daughter of Zion; behold your king is coming,
sitting on a donkey's colt!"
John 12:15 (See also Luke 19:29-38)

I have never been brave before
But I am the one He chose.
Feeling His fingers comb through my hair
I know He is safe.
I let Him mount and we begin to move together
Through the streets.
Where we are going I do not know,
But finally, I know Peace.
I hear His whispers as we pass through the crowd,
And the faces fade.
I am the donkey,
And He is the Lamb.
And I am not afraid anymore.

A Step Deeper In...

When Jesus searches the crowd to choose His ride, I want my hand raised. How about you? I invite you to pray with me, *"Here am I. Send me!" Isaiah 6:8*

Think about this truth, "I can trust that His leading me does not depend on my ability to see Him, only on my choice to follow even where I cannot see." Journal your thoughts.

Chapter 26

UNMOVED

My daughter, Rebekah, who loves horseback riding, explained to me the difference between riding bareback and riding in a saddle. She explained that when people ride bareback, their whole body must come into alignment with the horse. They are actually connected to the horse with nothing between the two of them, so the rider can feel the horse's every movement.

When people ride in a saddle they have more control. They have stirrups and a horn to hold onto and they are not as apt to fall. It's safer than riding bareback, but it's easy to slip out of alignment and the rider will miss the subtle, signaling movements of the horse that cannot be felt through the blanket and saddle. When riding bareback, nothing hinders the communication between the horse and his rider.

When Jesus calls us to follow Him, He is calling us to ride bareback. He will carry us where we need to go, but we have to let go of everything but Him. Those things that we hold onto to maintain control serve only to impede our sense of His leadership. The path He has us on is a path to the cross. It's a path of life, but it leads to life through death.

"If anyone would come after me, let him deny himself and take up his cross and follow me." (Mark 8:34 ESV) We are not here for earthly romance or riches, to have our needs met, to live in comfort or to gain approval from people. We are here to *die.*

Following Jesus in showing God's love to those for whom He died requires dying to oneself daily. And maybe someday it will require the radical obedience of literally dying physically for our faith in Jesus.

When Jesus walked this earth the reality of the cross was always before Him. He knew who He was, and that beyond the cross would be eternal life with the Father. Thus, He could set his face like flint to face death and all that death entailed. It was worth it to Him.

I think people way too often sugarcoat the gospel by focusing solely on the joy, peace, love, etc. that are offered us in Christ. Yes, it is all ours as a free gift. But if I am to fully experience intimacy with Christ, I am going to have to choose to ride bareback. I must let go of the controls that I think will keep me safe and follow the subtle movements of Jesus that lead me into dying to myself. In so doing I find life.

In Daniel 3 we read the story of Shadrach, Meshach and Abednego. They were taken as young men, along with Daniel, from their homes in Judah to Babylon where their names were changed, and they were indoctrinated with a new culture to enter the king's service.

The book of Daniel is fascinating, and it would be helpful to understanding this next poem if you could read chapters 1-3 first.

In your reading, notice that most of the action focuses on Daniel. He's the one in the spotlight—except for chapter 3. Shadrach, Meshach and Abednego seem to move in his shadow, until Daniel is moved away from them and placed in a high position of leadership. With their leader gone, they are called to make a choice—will they preserve their lives or choose to follow God regardless of what that will mean.

One thing I like about this story is that these men did not choose to stand for God because they knew God would prevent them from feeling pain. No. They chose to stand for God because they knew that whether they had to suffer a painful death or not, following God would be worth it. No matter what pain and suffering may be required, when we deny ourselves and take up our cross we know *Jesus is worth it all*. This is the good news of the gospel.

To Stand

*"They trusted in him and defied the king's command
and were willing to give up their lives rather than
serve or worship any god except their own God."*
Daniel 3:28b

Growing up unseen in a foreign land,
Moving in the shadow of another great man,
Today is the day I'm called to stand.
While others bow to save their lives
I cannot, will not sacrifice
My love for Christ.

The flames beside me roar of pain
But I will follow the Lamb who was slain...
Even if He is silent.

I will not bow to selfishness,
Unbelief or joylessness.
Whatever this blazing furnace means
I know the One who'll walk with me.
I CHOOSE TO STAND.

A Step Deeper In....

Horses scare me. Riding bareback scares me even more. Once, in a dream someone said to me "You don't have to try, but what if you were born to ride?"

Following Jesus with abandon is indeed what we were born for. Let's not miss it. Is God calling you in some way to let go of the saddle and trust Him more intimately than you ever have before?

Chapter 27

RADICAL

DENYING MYSELF, "TAKING UP MY CROSS," this is what Jesus says is required if I am to follow Him. He *will* lead me to places that require sacrifice.

"From the days of John the Baptist until now, the kingdom of heaven has suffered violence, and the violent take it by force." (Matthew 11:12 ESV) We lay hold of the kingdom of heaven by faith—forcefully, violently, with all our strength. It is not something we can lay hold of by staying clean and comfortable and passive.

Lest anyone think that I am saying we can gain the kingdom of heaven by our own strength, listen to a short story I once heard.

.... A mouse and an elephant march boldly over a bridge. Upon arriving on the other side, the mouse shouts triumphantly, "Wow! Didn't we shake that bridge?!"

The strongest mouse among us is still a mouse. I gain nothing through my own strength. But there is a reckless, forceful throwing myself upon Christ in faith that is violent. It requires sacrifice, letting go of something else to lay hold of Christ.

There are big sacrifices we are called to make, once or twice or a few times in our lives. But there are smaller daily sacrifices also. The calls to these are easy to miss because they are so ordinary and unexciting. They are not a call to something that the world will notice; only God will see. Only God will know you made a sacrifice for Him.

When I have my agenda set for the day and my husband calls needing my help with some task instead, will I sacrifice to follow Christ? When I am faced with the choice to tell of an injustice done or remain silent and protect another's reputation, will I sacrifice to follow Christ? When I have been hurt will I pull back and withhold love from the one who hurt me, or will I sacrifice to follow Christ?

When everything looks hopeless and like God is doing nothing, will I sacrifice to follow Christ and worship and trust Him anyway?

Sometimes these choices are fairly painless, and sometimes they require much of me, all my strength. But when God asked Abraham to sacrifice Isaac, one of those "all my strength" moments, Abraham got to see God like he never had seen Him before. This just seems to be the way God works.

After Job endured all his suffering and loss, he said, *"My ears had heard of you, but now my eyes have seen you."* (Job 42:5) That is what I want. I don't want to just hear of Jesus. I want to see Him, to know Him.

There was a time in my life when I stood in that hard place. Food was a big idol in my life for many years. It was my comfort. When I was stressed out I would retreat into the arms of chocolate chip cookies or other sweets.

In my mid-twenties, I found a large measure of freedom from my eating disorder and I no longer was consumed day in and day out with thoughts of food and weight. I no longer purged, and anyone who watched me would probably not think that I ate abnormally. I considered myself healed of the eating disorder.

However, at 35, I still turned to sweets for comfort and would eat maybe eight cookies or so to deal with stress. It was compulsive, and I knew it was sin—I was turning to food to meet the needs that God wanted to meet in my life.

There came a point where I felt God calling me deeper into knowing Him. I realized that I didn't have a clue how to receive comfort from Him. The many scriptures that speak of God comforting us—I hadn't experienced that from Him, and I wanted to. I wanted to know God as my Comforter.

One day I distinctly sensed God laying before me the choice—I could come to know Him as my Comforter, or I could continue running to food.

I knew that the only way I could give up this inferior comforter would be to completely give up sweets. This whole struggle may sound minor to you, but to me this was huge. It was a painful sacrifice.

In those first weeks, I experienced many times of crying out to God as I tried to resist the temptation to run to that old worthless comforter. I would offer my craving heart up to God as a sacrifice of worship and tell Jesus I wanted Him more. I would cry out to Him to reveal Himself to me as the One who would comfort me. Then I would open His Word and ask Him to speak to me.

And He did. That was the only way I could make this sacrifice—by laying hold of Christ and experiencing His loving comfort through His Word and His Presence. He truly did allow me to see Him like I never had been able to before.

As time went on there were times that I felt myself slipping back into dependence on certain foods and I had to repent and re-sacrifice and pray for God to reveal Himself to me afresh.

At times, I had to fight the lies that told me I was just being legalistic. Was I trusting in a strict rule to earn God's love, rather than resting in what Jesus did for me by dying for my sins? As I confessed my struggle to a wise friend, she confirmed to me that letting go of something that is taking God's place in our lives is not legalism. God had invited me to impose a strict boundary on myself, not to earn His love, but to free me from something that was blocking my view of the Love that I already possessed. I would encourage you also to find a wise friend who can help you stand in your choices to sacrifice something in order to lay hold of Someone.

The good news of the gospel is that I can be radical in sacrificing to follow Christ, because through sacrifice I will lay hold of the kingdom of heaven and I will know a fellowship with Christ that can be gained in no other way.

I Want to Know Christ

*"I want to know Christ—yes, to know the power of his resurrection
and participation in his sufferings, becoming like him in his death,
and so, somehow, attaining to the resurrection from the dead."*
Philippians 3:10,11

*"Then God said, "Take your son, your only son, whom you love—
Isaac—and go to the region of Moriah. Sacrifice him there..."*
Genesis 22:2a

When I lay my Isaac down
I do not understand.
I do not see salvation,
Just the knife within my hand.
The God Who gave laughter before,
The God I thought I knew,
Has disappeared and left me here
To find out that He's true.
When this world's loves are torn from me
I lie here crushed by grief.
Is He really Who He said He is,
My Savior, or...a thief?
I believe. LORD help my unbelief.
To whom else shall I go?
I cling to You and raise the knife,

I give You LORD...
My life.

Not a passive laying down,
A violent laying hold

Of God Who thrust the knife for me
Into His Son on Calvary.
Of Him Who cries "Lift up your eyes!
I Am the God Who sees!
When you lay your Isaac down
By your eyes I'll be seen."

"Abraham looked up and there in a
thicket he saw a ram..."
Genesis 22:13a

A Step Deeper In...

Is there a sacrifice God is calling you to make? It is a hard place to be. But I want to encourage you that you stand on the edge of breakthrough.

THE WAY

"Direct me in the path of your commands, for there I find delight."
Psalm 119:35

There is a path, a treasure map, that most mistake as rules.
A gift at birth from God, the secret passageway to pools
Where bubbling fountains of delight scattered along the way
Intoxicate me to press on deeper in each day.
A path of daily laying down, surrendering to Christ—
Not to chains of do's and don'ts, but to my Lover's voice.

"Jesus answered, "I am the way..."
John 14:6a

Chapter 28

FORGIVEN

Jesus. He is the Man who died for me and for you. It is intimidating to even try to write this chapter. How can I possibly portray the weight of who Jesus is?

Sometimes I get frustrated when people say, "God is good!" I think that is such a vague comment. It doesn't help me see Him. Tell me more! Tell me who He is so explicitly that I experience Him, taste Him, smell Him, feel His breath on my face. I want to *know* this Man.

As frustrated as I am with vague comments, I realize I can do no better at describing Jesus to you. You have to meet Him yourself. And that only happens one way; it comes through lifting your eyes to look into His eyes and receive the gift He is offering you. Total forgiveness.

Total forgiveness means all that stands between you and God, all your pride, all your selfishness, all your shame, all your sin is completely washed away. This is how we meet Jesus for the first time, and it's also how we continue to experience Him.

I remember as a young girl thinking that I didn't feel guilty enough for my sins. In an attempt to more fully grasp the weight of my depravity I constructed a large cardboard cross and wrote my sins on little papers, folding them neatly and tacking them on the cross.

As godly as that may appear, it was really an attempt to earn God's forgiveness by feeling guilty enough. The good news of the gospel is that this luscious, extravagant grace that Jesus pours out lavishly upon our heads is free! It is free even to those who can only see the tip of the iceberg of their own sin.

If you want to know Jesus, His blood shed for you is enough on day one, and it's enough fifty years later, when you think you haven't made any progress in your battle with sin. Jesus died for you because He wanted you, and He still wants you. His love for you is an *OCEAN!* Go on, take another step in!

THE MAN WHO DIED FOR ME

"looking to Jesus, the founder and perfecter of our faith,
who for the joy that was set before him endured the cross..."
Hebrew 12:2a ESV

How do I respond to The Man who died for me?
His bleeding, broken body hung naked on a tree?
My selfish heart cannot begin to grasp this mystery.
If only for a moment I could see what He can see.

My sin, like an iceberg, I only see the tip.
Jesus' love, like an ocean, covers all of it.
He bleeds for one who doesn't even know what lies below
The tiny tip that's visible to my pride-led soul.

Oh, Jesus, draw the tide back. Open up my eyes.
Ebb away the blindness that keeps me in disguise.
I cry out for your mercy, Lord. Let Your love touch my heart.
I need your power to set me free; melt each frozen part.
Let this entire iceberg be absorbed upon that tree
Where the nails were driven deep
And your flesh was torn for me.

For as the tide returns, it's come alive with heat,
Rushing to the holy place where God and man now meet.
A place of grace, bought with blood, a sea of fiery love.
Enough to touch my secret sins and instantly dissolve
Each frozen particle of fear, each hardened drop of pain,
Each sin I simply can't erase, each hurt that fell like rain.

The ocean waves leap up and roar, laughing with delight!
"Come dance with Me..." they seem to shout,
"come out into the Light!"
I Am a wild ocean, deeper still than your eyes see...
Way deeper than the ice that you've held out to Me.

So how do I respond to This Man who died for me?
His bleeding, broken body hung naked on a tree?
My selfish heart cannot begin to grasp this mystery.
If only for a moment I could see what He can see.

The love of God unfathomed, His sacrifice, my ransom.
For the joy set before Him He endured such misery.
This joy beyond description, now His at my salvation.
Delighting to show mercy, oh Lord, how can this be?
You see me as a treasure, one who'll bring you pleasure.
You poured out beyond measure...the price of Your own blood.

Who is this God who loves me? Who gave His life to save me?
Not simply out of pity, but He truly wanted me.

Amazing Love, I bow before Your mighty, holy throne.
Jesus, come and have my heart. I am now Yours alone.
Ocean waves of mercy, wash me through and through.
Melt away my sins and make me one with You.

As Your love melts me, layer upon layer,
The icy tower crumbles... my haughty eyes humbled.
I sink into Your waves' embrace,
My eyes transfixed upon your face, fascinated by Your grace.
Buoyed up I join Your dance, swept away in this holy romance.

The rushing current draws me deep
Where fluorescent colors of life You keep.
Mysteries ne'er seen by man unveiled to me now by Your hand.
Like a dolphin playing at sea I leap up again and shout to Thee,
"You are more than I ever dreamed You to be,
Holy! Holy! Holy!"

And then You draw me, Your strong undertow,
To another iceberg covered in snow.
To share the joy that I now know.

There is a man who died for thee.
Hung bleeding, broken on a tree.
He offers you this mystery.
Give Him your heart and you will see!

A Step Deeper In...

If you would like to give your life to Jesus, to follow Him and begin a relationship with Him, you must first receive the total forgiveness He offers you. Just pray something like this...

LORD Jesus,
I am a sinner in need of your mercy. Please forgive me for all my sins (past, present and future) and make me Your child. I believe that You died on the cross for my sins, taking my punishment. I receive your free gift of a clean heart and eternal life in heaven.
Thank-you Jesus. Amen."

SPILLED GLORY

*"But we have this treasure in jars of clay to show that this
all-surpassing power is from God and not from us."*
2 Corinthians 4:7

"Therefore, since we have such a hope, we are very bold."
2 Corinthians 3:12

An earthen vase, uplifted face,
Longing LORD for Your embrace.
Clumsy in my search for love...
The graceful path of Your Dove
Becomes obscured, hard to discern.
Your clear voice I want to learn.
I think I hear it, but I see
Pride and self all over me.
Am I worthy to outpour
The awesome beauty of my LORD?
No, I'm not. My sins they glare.
But what a shame if they should dare
To silence me and keep inside
The glory that we must not hide.
This earthen vessel I will tip,
In all of my awkwardness.
I'll fall down on my face and spill
The Living Water Jesus filled.
Pools and puddles everywhere,
The vessel's flaws don't matter here.
People splashing, drinking deep —
To think I almost chose to keep
Inside, the glory we must speak.

APPENDIX

Questions and Prayer Suggestions for Small Groups

Chapter 1 What angers you the most? Does your anger reveal what you care about the most? When you think of God's anger, do you think of it being directed at you or at what blocks you from Him? What is it in your life that blocks you from experiencing intimacy with Jesus?

Chapter 2 Do you relate to the woman in the poem who awaits plastic surgery? If so, how? What lies can you identify that you've believed about how God sees you? What scriptures can you use to replace the old lies with truth? Take time to pray together for revelation of how God sees you.

Chapter 3 Can you think of a time when you were spoken to by someone famous or well-respected? How did it make you feel? Can you share a time you experienced the awe of knowing that Jesus had just spoken something personally to you? Do you struggle with doubt that God will speak to you through the Bible? Are there any scriptures you've found that help build your faith in this area? Take time to pray together for increased faith that God will speak to you personally, and for increased hunger for His Word.

Chapter 4 Why do you think God asks us to sing to Him? Why does He ask us to sing a "new song?" (*Psalm 96:1*) Could you share a memory where you experienced the joy of being loved by a small child? Can you imagine Jesus feeling that same joy over your expressed love for Him? Take time to worship Jesus together. Take turns telling Him what He means to you.

Chapter 5 How do you know when someone has truly heard your heart? Does pouring out your sorrows to God come easy or hard for you? Can you identify anything in your life that stands in the way of your pouring out your sorrows to God? Take time to pray for each other that these barriers will crumble.

Chapter 6 Can you recall an experience of being chosen? Would you like to share it? Can you recall an experience you've had in your relationship with the LORD that has helped you grow in your knowledge that He has chosen you? Are there experiences that you've had that impede your ability to believe this truth? Take time to pray for each other's healing in this area.

Chapter 7 Have you ever felt truly known by someone? When you think about Jesus truly knowing you, what emotions surface? Are there thoughts you feel that you could begin to express to Jesus in prayer, knowing that He already knows all about them, and loves you? Pray together that Jesus will reveal to you how completely you are known and yet how deeply you are loved. Pray over each other the prayer Paul prayed in Ephesians 3:16-21.

Chapter 8 Can you share a time when you experienced great loss? What truths of scripture brought you comfort? Jesus not only cared deeply about your grief, but He died to break the power of death. Take time to pray over each other, for revelation of the depth of Jesus' compassion as we walk through grief.

Chapter 9 What do you think God sees as success? How do you think God views you in the midst of your worst failures?

Take time to pray for each other to more fully experience the realization of God's amazing grace.

Chapter 10 Do you relate to the deaf and mute man of Mark 7? What about Jesus stands out to you in this story? Can you relate to the feelings expressed in this poem? Have you experienced feelings of shame for not being able to hear God's voice, or fear of speaking freely what you think and feel? Take time to pray for each other, for Jesus to open your spiritual senses to hear His voice more clearly, and to speak freely without fear. Tell Jesus you want to know Him.

Chapter 11 Do you have a testimony of healing that you'd like to share? It could be your own, or about someone you know. What has Christ purchased for us on the cross? What does it mean to you that Jesus has given us His name? Take time to ask together in Jesus' name for the things you need.

Chapter 12 Can you share a testimony of how God set you free in an area of previous bondage? Can you identify any idols in your life? Sometimes confessing sin to God and another believer is the first step to finding freedom. Take time to pray for each other for freedom from bondage. Pray for God to expose the lies that are maintaining any idols in your lives and pray that He will make His truth known to you.

Chapter 13 Can you identify with how Mary felt in John 11? How so? What stands out to you the most about how Jesus responded to Mary? Take time to pray together that God will give you revelation of how He responds to your emotions when He seems silent.

Chapter 14 What does it mean to you that Jesus would fight for you? Read 2 Corinthians 4:18 together. How does one fix their eyes on what is unseen? Read together Isaiah 49:25. What has the enemy stolen from you? Pray together for God to "contend with those who contend with you", retrieve what has been stolen, and save your children.

Chapter 15 How do you run into the safety of Jesus? In your joys do you think to search for Jesus' eyes? What holds you back from trusting Him? Pray together for God to help you trust Him like a child.

Chapter 16   What is your understanding of God's grace? Is there something you are pursuing that has shifted your gaze away from Jesus? Pray together for an ever-growing understanding of the grace we've been given in Christ. Pray that Jesus will capture your gaze afresh.

Chapter 17   How do you respond to feeling out of control? What truths anchor you at those times? If you have taken the time to write out the hope you profess, would you be willing to share it with the group? Pray together that God will ground you securely in the truth that Jesus Christ is all you need.

Chapter 18   How has God restored your soul? Where do you sense Him working in your life right now? Pray for each other, for the areas where you sense God currently working, or where you feel the need for further restoration.

Chapter 19   What things distract you from the Lord? What line from this poem stirs something in your own heart? Take time to pray together. Thank God for how He pursues us even in the face of our waywardness. Ask Him to give you a deeper revelation of His passionate pursuing love for you.

Chapter 20   What is romance? How have you experienced romance in your relationship with Jesus? What spoke to you the most from this chapter? What things can one do to cultivate romance in their relationship with Jesus? Read Matthew 22:36,37 together and pray that Jesus will help you love Him with all your heart and soul and mind.

Chapter 21   Can you identify any lies that have been for you like "layer upon layer of black tape placed over the head of a flash-light"? What steps can you take to remove those layers and lay hold of the truth? Pray together for discernment to recognize the lies of the enemy, for strength to reject those lies, and for faith to lay hold of the truth.

Chapter 22 How have you experienced the darkness of not knowing Christ at all, compared to the darkness of not yet knowing Him fully? What "mining techniques" do you use? What holds you back from digging deep to discover the treasures of more intimately knowing God? Pray for each other, that those things would no longer hold you back. Pray that God would give you faith to believe that as you seek Him He will reveal Himself to you.

Chapter 23 Have you ever had a moment of discovering the delight of how God feels for you? Do you remember anything that led up to that moment of discovery? How did it change your life? Has it become a distant memory? Take time to pray together for ever-deepening and ever-fresh revelation of Jesus' delight in you.

Chapter 24 Is there a "field of dirt, ripe for seed" that God has set before you? What step could you take today to plant a seed? Pray for each other, that you would "...hear the word, retain it, and by persevering produce a crop." Luke 8:15

Chapter 25 What has helped you most in discerning the leading of the Holy Spirit? Does the awareness of the Holy Spirit's power within you change your personality? If so, how? If you lived in constant awareness of that fully accessible, powerful Presence, how would your days look different?

Chapter 26 Is there a saddle horn you need to let go of in order to be able to follow the subtle movements of Jesus as He leads you? What ways have you sensed Him leading you to take up your cross and lay down your own life? Pray for each other for revelation that Jesus is worth it—no matter what sacrifice you are called to make.

Chapter 27 Has Jesus asked you to sacrifice anything to follow Him? Have you ever made a sacrifice that led to seeing God like you never had before? Is there something good that is taking God's place in your life? Take time to pray for each other for faith that is fierce in laying hold of the knowledge of Christ.

Chapter 28   What spoke to you the most in this chapter? Have you ever struggled with wondering if you feel guilty enough for your sin to truly be forgiven? Do you feel a need for greater assurance of Jesus' total forgiveness? Take time to pray together, to thank Jesus for what this gift of forgiveness cost Him. Pray for greater revelation of your need for Him and of His delight in washing you clean.

In Conclusion

Do you ever let the awareness of your own brokenness disqualify you from telling others the good news of the gospel? If those fears were taken away, what would you do to spill out "the glory that we must not hide"? Pray together for boldness. Pray for the Holy Spirit to fill you afresh with this "uncontainable fountain of glorious living water." And then go forth from here "with the reckless joy of a child unleashing a puppy as they race down the seashore and splash into the waves."